New Museums   Raul A. Barreneche

New Museums	Raul A. Barreneche	

Contents

Introduction

The Age of the Museum

The beginning of this new century will surely go down in history as a golden age for the museum. Since an ongoing boom in museum building started in the 1990s, the public has greeted openings of new museums and expansions of older institutions with a previously unimaginable level of fanfare and excitement. Traveling exhibitions have become certifiable blockbusters as popular as hit movies and musicals. Tickets for the biggest shows sell out months in advance; visitors are willing to line up for hours, whether to see Matisse's paintings or Jackie Kennedy's ball gowns. The way museums now market themselves is a big reason for their surge in popularity. No longer elitist institutions, they vie with theme parks and other mass-market entertainment for a slice of the public's leisure time and disposable income. But an even bigger motive is, quite simply, the architecture. Crowds come for the building as much as for the objects on display inside—a phenomenon that took off in 1997 when Frank Gehry's Guggenheim Museum in Bilbao and the Getty Center in Los Angeles, designed by Richard Meier, opened almost simultaneously. Since that momentous year, dozens of museums have commissioned the world's top architects to create new buildings, hoping to echo the success of the Guggenheim and the Getty. As a result, museums more than any other building type have become the architectural barometers of our era. ____ Gehry's Guggenheim completely turned the tables on the way the public perceived museums. A runaway success, the new Guggenheim demonstrated that a single building could energize an institution and fuel the revitalization of an entire city and region. Other institutions and other cities in need of a turnaround wanted to replicate the "Bilbao effect"—that is, putting up a museum with architectural credentials to boost a civic and cultural image and change economic fortunes. Never mind that Gehry's Guggenheim was a hit because of a felicitous coming together of program, place, and client. Museum directors thought they saw the writing on the wall: Build it—a significant piece of architecture, that is—and they will come. ____ Since Bilbao opened less than a decade ago, museums have sprung up in every corner of the globe. They come in every shape and size, appeal to every conceivable taste, and cover a dizzying array of subjects. As historian Victoria Newhouse notes in her excellent book *Towards a New Museum*, "One intriguing aspect of the current proliferation of museums is the 'museumification' of seemingly every phenomenon known to humanity, from Sverre Fehn's Glacier Museum in Norway to Hans Hollein's Vulcania...a museum about volcanoes in France's Auvergne region" (page 94).[1] ____ Glaciers and volcanoes are just the beginning. The past few years have seen the birth of museums dedicated to handicrafts (New York's Museum of Arts & Design, formerly the American Craft Museum, which hopes to move into Brad Cloepfil's contentious renovation of Edward Durell Stone's lollipop-studded Huntington Hartford building on Columbus Circle); comic strips and children's book illustrations (a museum dedicated to the *Peanuts* of cartoonist Charles M. Schulz in Santa Rosa, California, and the Eric Carle Museum of Picture Book Art in Amherst, Massachusetts, founded by the illustrator of the classic children's book *The Very Hungry Caterpillar*); paper-making (Shigeru Ban's Paper Art Museum in Japan, page 44); and glass (the Museum of Glass in Tacoma, Washington, designed by Arthur Erickson, with a crystalline bridge by artist Dale Chihuly). An International Balloon Museum is rising near Albuquerque, New Mexico, and a museum dedicated to the world's largest collection of automobiles is due to break ground in Tacoma in 2005. There's a Museum of the Earth in Ithaca, New York, by Weiss/Manfredi Architects and a museum by Juan Navarro Baldeweg near Spain's Altamira caves (page 150) with a re-creation of the famous and fragile Paleolithic caves. There are Jewish museums in cities from New York to Sydney (though Daniel Libeskind's in Berlin, page 120, is architecturally the most prominent) and Holocaust museums in dozens of other spots from Melbourne, Australia, to Saint Louis, Missouri. There's a Museum of Fantasy in Bernried, Germany, designed by Behnisch,

Left: Frank Gehry's Guggenheim Bilbao raised the stakes on museum design when it opened in 1997. ___ Right: Richard Meier's one-billion-dollar Getty Center opened its doors the same year.

Behnisch & Partner, and a Museum of Sex in Manhattan, which settled into more inconspicuous digs after abandoning an ambitious design by the hip New York architecture firm SHoP. ___ In the realm of traditional fine art, collections are ever more focused. There's no longer much point in simply speaking of an art museum when there are entire institutions devoted to modern art, contemporary art, and folk art, not to mention painting, sculpture, and photography. There are more monographic museums dedicated to a single artist—such as Mario Botta's Jean Tinguely Museum in Basel and Gigon/Guyer's Liner Museum in Appenzell, Switzerland (page 22), which is dedicated to the father-and-son painters Carl Walter Liner and Carl August Liner. These museums build on the strengths of earlier monographic landmarks: Richard Gluckman's gritty but slick Andy Warhol Museum in Pittsburgh and Renzo Piano's sumptuous Cy Twombly Gallery in Houston. ___ It is not just trustees and mayors fueling the museum-building frenzy. Private benefactors are pitching in to put up sumptuous buildings for their collections; some christen them foundations, others set up full-fledged museums. In 2004, the Collection Frieder Burda opened a crisp white gallery building designed by Richard Meier in Baden Baden, Germany, while the Langen Foundation unveiled its dramatic new home, designed by Tadao Ando, on a former NATO missile site near Düsseldorf. Collectors Shelly and Donald Rubin set up the Rubin Museum of Art in a renovated department store in downtown Manhattan to display their collection of more than 1,500 works of Himalayan art dating from the twelfth century. These collectors are betting that their money and good intentions, along with a bit of architecture and a hopefully decent collection, will be enough to draw an audience. It is a risky proposition when the public is saturated with museums at every turn; just skimming the tally of new and forthcoming projects is enough to make your head spin. ___ Well-established museums are spawning offspring in multiple locations. The Imperial War Museum North, designed by Daniel Libeskind in Manchester (page 80), is one of three outposts of England's Imperial War Museum, which also occupies a Norman Foster–designed air museum in Duxford and a classical building in London. Most famously, of course, are the multiple progeny of the Solomon R. Guggenheim Museum in New York. Its locations in Berlin, designed by Richard Gluckman, and Venice (the Peggy Guggenheim Collection, displayed in the former home of founder Solomon Guggenheim's niece) showcase the museum's holdings around the world. Its Las Vegas branch, a strange-bedfellow joint operation with St. Petersburg's venerable Hermitage Museum, is still open, although a stand-alone Guggenheim branch closed early in 2003. Designed by Rem Koolhaas, the Hermitage Guggenheim Museum's Cor-Ten steel structure sits inside the ostentatious Venetian casino resort in surreal juxtaposition. Of course, Gehry's Bilbao satellite, still the most successful of the Guggenheim Foundation's expansion adventures, continues to draw the crowds that have transformed this gritty industrial town in Spain's Basque country into a destination for the globetrotting cultural set. ___ One wonders whether such a glut of establishments waters down the prestige or cachet of museums, or if the boom is democratizing and demystifying institutions, making them more accessible to a wider public. Museums with multiple locations suffer from a different problem: one collection, many buildings. On a world art tour, it's possible to see the same shows circulating through several different venues. (It happened to me when I went to Bilbao and stumbled upon the same Robert Rauschenberg retrospective I had already seen in New York.) It seems that any institution with the will, the collection, and the means can build itself a museum. If it is built, though, will the crowds come? For some of these offbeat institutions, that remains to be seen. ___ This book features more than two dozen of the most important museums and exhibition spaces built around the world in recent years. Nearly all of them are new buildings, but the standout additions included here, most notably the Museum of Modern Art's Yoshio Taniguchi–designed expansion (page 194), acknowledge the need for many museums to expand their facilities when they are pressed for space or need to add modern-day amenities to remain competitive on the global scene. Some projects, such as I.M. Pei's now iconic pyramid in the Cour Napoleon of the Louvre, are more reorganizations and re-accommodations than outright alterations to existing buildings, which can be more contentious than building a new museum from scratch. (Imagine the outcry if Pei had tried to add directly onto the Louvre's expansive wings.) In *Towards a New Museum*, Newhouse charts some of the museum world's most controversial and complicated expansion programs in the provocatively titled chapter "Wings That Don't Fly (And Some That Do)." As Newhouse points out: "No matter how problematic museum architecture may be, adding to it can prove more so. Museum expansion is generally perceived as the direct result of a need for additional space, but other, often extraneous considerations can influence the decision to take on these consuming and costly projects. Richard Oldenburg, director of MoMA from 1972 to 1994, notes that for one thing, new people usually want new things, and physical expansion is a way for trustees, or a director, to leave an indelible imprint."[2] ___ The twenty-year battle, still ongoing, to expand the Whitney Museum of American Art beyond its 1966 Marcel Breuer–designed home in New York may be as much about adding space as it is about changing the museum's identity through architecture (page 13). Its Upper East Side neighbors and New York City's Landmarks Preservation Commission succeeded in stopping a 1985 behemoth addition by Michael Graves that would have required the demolition of several adjoining nineteenth-century townhouse. Graves's gargantuan scheme would have subsumed Breuer's original into a dizzying assemblage of Brutalism meets Postmodernism. After it became clear that Graves's scheme, even though redesigned several times, would never succeed, the Whitney scrapped the plan. In 1998, the museum quietly expanded its offices, conference rooms, and library into two neighboring townhouses subtly and gracefully renovated by architect Richard Gluckman, the master of stealth minimalism. Hardly anyone noticed, and the museum carried on—though it kept acquiring works and soon needed additional space to house its growing permanent collection, which had ballooned by more than 65 percent in ten years. ___ The expansion controversy resurfaced in 2001, when the Whitney's board announced plans for another addition by Rem Koolhaas, an architect not known for his sensitivity to history—or to community boards. Koolhaas made two flamboyant proposals that would have cost $200 million to build. In 2003, the Whitney scrapped those plans, only to announce a new, more restrained scheme by Renzo Piano in 2004. Piano's proposal calls for a subtle cubic glass volume set behind the original Breuer building and the townhouses renovated by Gluckman, rising taller than the Breuer wing and connected to it with luminous bridges at each level. As of this writing, the museum was committed to Piano's scheme; whether this design will actually be built remains to be seen—though one can imagine that the board and the architects have learned their lessons by now. ___ The Whitney is certainly not alone in its tangled plans for expansion, though its story is perhaps more tortured than that of comparable institutions. New York's Guggenheim Museum had its own experience with angry preservationists, critics, scholars, and neighborhood groups when it presented plans designed by Charles Gwathmey and Robert Siegel for an addition to its iconic Frank Lloyd Wright building. Many likened Gwathmey Siegel's none-too-subtle structure to a rectilinear "tank" behind Wright's curvilinear "toilet."[3] The addition that was eventually built was a slimmer, more discrete slab clad in gridded limestone; but for many, Wright's only New York building was forever marred. ___ Long before the opening of

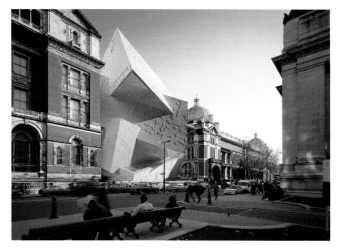

Left: The Cor-Ten facade of Rem Koolhaas's Hermitage Guggenheim Museum in Las Vegas. ___ Right: London's Victoria & Albert Museum with its never-realized Daniel Libeskind extension.

his Jewish Museum in Berlin and his master plan for the World Trade Center site in lower Manhattan, Daniel Libeskind proposed a competition-winning extension to London's august Victoria & Albert Museum. Known as the Spiral, Libeskind's jagged, aggressive design looked like "a gargantuan pile of rock candy," in the words of *New Yorker* architecture critic Paul Goldberger.[4] After almost a decade of waiting for funds to be raised and construction to start, the museum's trustees announced in September 2004 that they were canceling the project. The museum cited the rejection of requests for necessary public funding from the Arts Council England and the Heritage Lottery Fund as the reason it was pulling the plug on the project after so many years, and after private money had been raised to build it. ___ Officially, that is the case. But underlying the demise of the project is the fact that when it was first unveiled, nearly ten years ago, the scheme caused a huge public outcry in England, where Prince Charles had been trying his hardest to shape architectural taste. (Who could forget his famous "monstrous carbuncle" comment about a proposed addition to the National Gallery on Trafalgar Square?) As in New York, local residents of South Kensington opposed the deconstructivist addition to the genteel Victorian exterior, despite the endorsement of English Heritage and the Royal Fine Arts Commission. Libeskind's aborted proposal under-scores the external forces at play on architects designing additions to well-loved institutions. It may be one thing to design an expansion that meets with the curators' and trustees' approval; it's quite another to get endorsement from regulato-ry agencies and the general public. ___ Renzo Piano seems to have mastered the art of the deal when it comes to adding onto existing institutions, especially historic buildings in residential neighborhoods. Besides his newest proposal for the Whitney Museum, which is still in the earliest stages of development and approval, Piano's subtle expansion of New York's Morgan Library is currently well on its way: It is expected to open in early 2006. Piano's scheme—a large underground structure and three delicate glass-and-steel pavilions inserted among the library and museum's three historic buildings—sailed through the approvals process, winning praise along the way from the New York City Landmarks Preservation Commission, the Municipal Arts Society, and the local chapter of the American Institute of Architects. In Atlanta, the Pritzker Prize–winning Piano is adding onto a landmark of late twentieth-century Modernism: Richard Meier's High Museum of Art. Piano's expansion will more than double the High's exhibition space and will add many of those ameni-ties that are now requirements, not luxuries: a restaurant, a café, a museum store, and an education center. ___ The addi-tions featured in this book reveal a variety of attitudes toward adapting history to suit the needs of the modern-day muse-um. The Centre PasquArt in Biel, Switzerland, expanded by the Swiss rationalist Roger Diener (page 100), and Dutch architect Abel Cahen's more radical addition to the Van Abbemuseum in Eindhoven (page 182) represent a straightfor-ward impetus for expansion: too many artifacts, too little space. Both architects renovated the existing institutions and then added new wings to the original buildings. Diener's approach was to distinguish his building from the original, a former hospital occupied by the private contemporary art foundation since the late 1980s, through abstraction and quiet modernity. He added a stark stone box with minimal articulation to the eastern end of the facility that keeps a physical distance from the classical structures to the west. There is no mistaking old and new, as is also the case with Cahen's

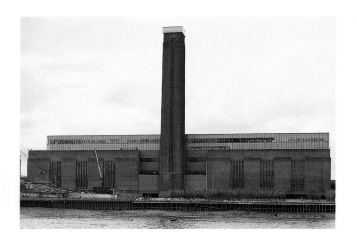

Left: Herzog & de Meuron's transformation of London's Bankside Power Station into the Tate Modern owed much to the original building's dramatic scale and location. ___ Right: In 1987, Gae Aulenti renovated a Parisian train station and turned it into the renowned Musée d'Orsay. ___ Opposite, left: OpenOffice's renovation of a cookie-box factory provided ample space for Dia:Beacon's large-scale sculptures. ___ Opposite, right: Michael Maltzan and Cooper, Robertson & Partners revamped an old stapler factory for MoMA QNS.

Van Abbemuseum. That institution was originally housed in a prim 1930s red brick building with a clock tower. Cahen's expansion, which is much larger than the original structure, makes no effort to disguise its relative youth. The architect clad the hulking addition—an aggressive form with an angular tower intended to dwarf the original clock tower and assert its prominence within the composition—in an almost pixilated pattern of gray slate squares. The connections between the two structures are underground; on the outside, they stand apart physically and ideologically. The new wing has a modern spirit to it and communicates the message that the museum is not just adding space; it is embracing the future and all its repercussions on the museum, from updated technology to a user-friendly attitude. Indeed, for institutions looking to expand their buildings, the message communicated by the architecture is an important consideration. Will it signal an embrace of the past or a nod to the future? More of the same or something completely different? ___ Norman Foster's striking design for the Great Court at the venerable British Museum in London (page 66) is both. Foster's subtle but dramatic transformation of the once bleak interior courtyard vacated by the British Library when it moved to Saint Pancras enhances the solid classicism of the original museum and adds a completely new and modern twist to the stately dowager of Bloomsbury. To call it a renovation is to shortchange Foster's project, which in essence covered the huge internal courtyard with a dramatic curved and vaulted lattice-like skylight around the classical drum of the preserved Reading Room at the center. Physically, the project brings light into the center of the vast museum and discretely adds much-needed modern-day amenities such as a café, restrooms, and a shop. Psychologically, the design creates a focal point to the original building and helps organize the flow of visitors who flock to see the Elgin Marbles, the Rosetta Stone, and other treasures. There is now a functional spot from which to launch one's visit through the museum. Sometimes, a grand open space—such as Foster's revamped Great Court or I.M. Pei's subterranean lobbies beneath the Louvre's pyramid—can transform a weary institution more than extra gallery space would. A bigger, better lobby may not draw people to a museum, but it certainly improves their experience and, therefore, their impressions of the institution. ___ Austrian architects Ortner & Ortner's design for Vienna's museum quarter (page 128) takes the ideas of addition and renovation to a huge urban scale. The architects were responsible for the overall plan to transform an array of baroque buildings, formerly the imperial stables, into a creative hub of art museums and other cultural organizations. Into this grand architectural compound the designers inserted two distinctly contemporary structures: the white stone-clad Leopold Museum and the all-black Museum of Modern Art Ludwig Foundation. The Ortners opted for Modernist abstraction as a way to distinguish old and new in such a historically charged context. The strategy works: The new museum blocks are integrated into the overall urban plan of the museum quarter, and thereby into the existing architecture, but they remain visually distinct. ___ The adaptive reuse of historic structures in contemporary museums is becoming a viable alternative for space-hungry institutions. Private galleries, especially in New York, have been reappropriating old industrial spaces for years,

first in SoHo and more recently in Chelsea; but mainstream museums have not followed suit so quickly. Older buildings—like the former print works that now houses the Massachusetts Museum of Contemporary Art (Mass MoCA) in North Adams—are not precisely blank canvases; but they offer big, ready-made spaces quite suitable for large-scale contemporary works of art. One of the most dramatic adaptations of a historic building is Gae Aulenti's 1987 renovation of a 1900 Beaux Arts train station in Paris into a landmark museum of nineteenth-century art: the Musée d'Orsay. Aulenti took Victor Laloux's stunning Gare d'Orsay, with its soaring skylit vault and gilded cast-iron ornament, and turned it into a functioning museum with semiautonomous gallery pavilions flanking its dramatic central nave. ___ Aulenti's Musée d'Orsay was one of the first major museums to take up residence in a repurposed building. In the years since its opening, institutions of various stripes have followed a similar path. One of the most notable recent examples is London's Tate Modern, housed in a vast 1960s power station refitted by Swiss architects Jacques Herzog and Pierre de Meuron. It's hard to imagine the architects being able to create such an enormous and prominent landmark in the middle of London if they had been building a new museum from scratch. Instead, they benefited from the dramatic scale and imposing urban profile of the former Bankside Power Station on the south bank of the Thames. Inside, they inherited the remarkable scale of the Turbine Hall—a vast, towering void that has become the museum's greatest attraction, especially when contemporary artists take over the space to add temporary site-specific installations, many of which have become blockbusters in their own right. ___ In Beacon, New York, about one hour north of Manhattan, an old industrial plant where Nabisco cookie boxes were once printed is now the stunning home of Dia:Beacon. The site is an outpost of the New York–based Dia Foundation, which has collected work by the most important minimalist artists, such as Richard Serra, Dan Flavin, Carl Andre, and Donald Judd. Many of the works are huge, like Serra's *Torqued Ellipses*, so the jaw-dropping vastness of the old industrial structure works perfectly with the art displayed within its whitewashed walls. Row upon row of sawtooth skylights admit so much natural light that even on an overcast day the galleries positively glow. Again, one wonders if the architects—in this case the young New York firm OpenOffice, working in collaboration with artist Robert Irwin—could have created such a successful setting for art, particularly the difficult large-scale work collected by the Dia, if they were to attempt to build a museum from the ground up instead of adapting a sympathetic old building. ___ The Museum of Modern Art has just moved into its gleaming new quarters in Manhattan; but while the building was in construction, MoMA moved across the East River to Long Island City, Queens, where the museum took up temporary residence in an old Swingline Stapler factory. Los Angeles architect Michael Maltzan and the New York firm Cooper, Robertson & Partners revamped the old factory, dubbed MoMA QNS, adding a ramped entry sequence, a gift shop, a café, and galleries, and brought the structure up to par environmentally so that the museum's priceless works could be properly stored and exhibited. Familiar masterworks such as Picasso's *Les Demoiselles d'Avignon* and van Gogh's *Starry Night* took on new life in the galleries created beneath the old factory's towering ceilings. The scale and raw industrial quality of these spaces recalls the character of New York's contemporary galleries, now ensconced in old warehouses and taxi garages in western Chelsea. That a mainstream institution such as MoMA would embrace such a gritty unpolished space seems plausible only because it was a temporary move, but the possibilities afforded by housing museums in a repurposed building are tantalizing. Indeed, as more institutions confront the need for added space, transforming old train stations, warehouses, and factories into galleries could become a more common paradigm. ___ It is clear that curators and directors are giving much thought to the evolution of their institutions, given the fundamental changes at play in the museum world. Nicholas Serota, director of the Tate Gallery in London, noted the dilemma facing today's art museums in a lecture he gave in 1996: "What do we expect from museums of modern art and the end of the twentieth century? We may agree that the encyclopedic and dictionary functions of the museum are neither achievable nor desirable. But there is less general agreement on how to balance the interests of the artist, the curator, and the visitor. Some of the larger institutions have begun to explore new approaches. However, the most stimulating developments have occurred in smaller museums, where the sense of institutional responsibility towards conventional expectations is less pressing."[5] ___ Serota cited quirkier, nontraditional organizations—such as the Hallen für Neue Kunst in Schaffhausen, Switzerland, and Donald Judd's museum complex in Marfa, Texas—among the more innovative institutions. Indeed, smaller noncollecting institutions have proven to be fertile ground for architectural innovation. From Rem Koolhaas's Kunsthal Rotterdam to Zaha Hadid's Rosenthal Center for Contemporary Art in Cincinnati (page 36) and Peter Cook and Colin Fournier's Kunsthaus Graz in Graz, Austria (page 50), these organizations have continued to commission provocative buildings, perhaps because they are more nimble and unencumbered by the institutional baggage of larger, more established museums. ___ Serota touched on the fact that museums are changing from within, redefining themselves and their role in society in the process. There is, however, no single clear direction that has emerged—so the architectural resolution of these ideas remains as varied as the thinking on the part of the institutions. Some directors—along with many architects—believe that the museum building is itself an artifact and perhaps the most important work in a collection. Others think that, inside and out, museums should be neutral boxes: What matters most is the content, not the container. The buildings featured in this book make strong arguments for both schools of thought. Among other projects, Kengo Kuma's Museum of Hiroshige Ando (page 136), Yoshio Taniguchi's Gallery of Horyuji Treasures (page 14) and his recent expansion of MoMA (page 194), Tadao Ando's Modern Art Museum of Fort Worth (page 58), Shigeru Ban's Paper Art Museum, Herzog & de Meuron's Schaulager (page 72), and Álvaro Siza's Serralves Museum of Contemporary Art (page 176) make the case for museums that don't aim to be attention-grabbing works of art. They are neutral, but certainly not mute. Other buildings, notably Steven Holl's Kiasma Museum of Contemporary Art in Helsinki (page 188), Hans Hollein's Vulcania Museum in France (page 94), and Santiago Calatrava's eye-popping addition to the Milwaukee Art Museum (page 156) offer a different approach: signature buildings that, even if they don't overshadow the objects on display inside, position themselves as the museum's most visible work of art. The debate between neutral and not-neutral museum buildings is hardly a new one, and it does not show signs of resolution. ___ The term "museum" used to conjure up images of grand institutions in cosmopolitan capitals: the Metropolitan in New York, the Louvre in Paris, the Victoria & Albert in London. These encyclopedic repositories of artistic treasures had an exclusive, elitist image that was hard to shake. The London architect Ian Ritchie, who designed the glass towers of Madrid's Reina Sofía Art Center, summarizes the fundamental shifts in the identity of the contemporary museum: "Museums have been revolutionized by the desire, indeed the perceived need, to attract as many visitors as possible. The days when they were frequented by the researcher, the odd school party, and the Sunday family outing are very distant indeed....This revolution has had a dramatic impact on the spatial programs of museums, on the very nature of their organization, and indeed, in many instances, on the very role for which they were created. Most dramatic, perhaps, is the ability of these buildings to simply accommodate the flow of visitors, and from a marketing view, hold them long enough without boring them so that they spend at the book store and shops, but short enough to allow more visitors in."[6] ___ Ritchie notes that such purposeful increases in visitor numbers have forced existing museums to renovate just to accommodate bigger crowds. This factor, coupled with multifunction spaces open to the public beyond the museum's

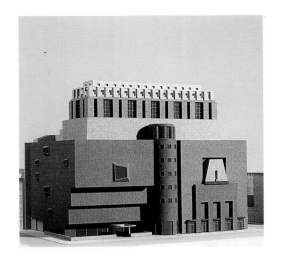  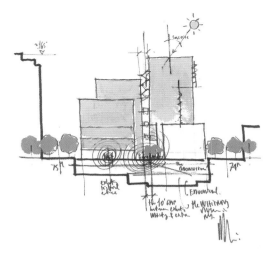

Left: Michael Graves's 1985 proposed addition to the Whitney Museum of American Art would have appended Postmodernism to Marcel Breuer's 1966 Brutalist structure. —— Center: Rem Koolhaas's flamboyant 2001 proposal was ultimately too expensive for the Whitney to approve. —— Right: Renzo Piano's 2004 design will add a cubic glass volume and bridges to Breuer's original.

own operating hours, has had a ripple effect on the architectural programming inside: bigger lobbies, wider hallways, and more space for restaurants, temporary exhibition galleries, lecture halls, conference facilities, and libraries, among other trappings now de rigueur in the modern museum. —— Architect Denise Scott Brown has noted the architectural changes in the programming of museums brought about by the shift to accessibility and entertainment: "I think something else is happening in museums now. In the museums we designed we had to provide a great deal of nonmuseum space. Today's museum is part restaurant, part shop, and part education department; it is full of lecture halls, conference rooms, and computer spaces, where visitors can find information away from the paintings. Museums want to offer people different ways of knowing art."[7] —— Indeed, across the board, museums are recasting themselves as accessible, family-friendly places of entertainment as much as centers of education or enlightenment. (Perhaps an anomaly among today's more populist institutions, Meier's $1 billion Getty acropolis did little to advance the view of museums as culturally snobbish ivory towers. The museum tried its best to portray itself as engaged with the masses, putting up banners in ethnically diverse neighborhoods across Los Angeles; but the building's hilltop perch high above a Los Angeles freeway still made it seem aloof and elitist.) Perhaps an extreme example, the Museum of American Folk Art's new facility by New York architects Tod Williams and Billie Tsien (page 114) captures the warm fuzzy feeling of the friendlier, more accessible new generation of museum. Located next door to the mighty MoMA, Williams and Tsien's building is purposely cozy, almost domestic in scale—in fact, the architects refer to it as a "house of folk art." Of course, the handcrafted, homespun nature of the art on display in this particular museum and the smallness of its tight urban site make its warm, tactile design and its almost residential scale appropriate, even necessary. But it is certainly not the only institution to eschew architectural pyrotechnics for comfort and familiarity. David Chipperfield's River & Rowing Museum in Henley on Thames, UK (page 162), has a similarly intimate scale and feeling. It is rather like visiting a museum housed in an old boat shed or someone's boat-filled garage. —— There seems to be no end in sight for the museum boom. The next few years will see even more new buildings and major expansions come to light, as projects by the world's leading architects that have been years in the making are finally finished. More buildings will give us the chance to gauge the evolution of the museum typology and the changing thoughts and attitudes of trustees, directors, curators, and the general public about what, exactly, the museum is and how it should operate in the world.

Japanese architect Yoshio Taniguchi's special brand of minimalism—crisp, exactingly crafted volumes of exquisite proportion—is in evidence on a grand scale in the Museum of
Modern Art's expansion in New York (page 195). One of the
buildings that impressed MoMA trustees when considering

Taniguchi & Associates	1999	
Gallery of Horyuji Treasures		
Tokyo, Japan		

architects for the coveted addition to their museum was the Gallery of Horyuji Treasures, part of the Tokyo National
Museum. Taniguchi's design anchors a corner of Ueno Park with a delicate glass box wrapped in a thin metal portico. The
museum is a suitably discrete addition to an architecturally eclectic cultural complex that includes the National
Museum's main building, an imposing neoclassical structure with Japanese roofline, built in the 1930s; a traditional
Japanese garden pavilion; and, most significantly, the museum's Asian wing, housed in a Brutalist concrete building
designed by Taniguchi's father, Yoshiro, in 1968. Nearby is the National Museum of Western Art, designed by Le Corbusier
in 1959. ___ Covering 43,000 square feet (4,031 square meters), the younger Taniguchi's structure is dedicated primarily to the Horyuji Treasures, a collection of more than three hundred artifacts mainly from the seventh and eighth centuries that were donated to the Japanese imperial household by the Horyuji Temple in 1878. Many pieces of the collection
are considered national cultural treasures. The gallery exterior is visually light, with a delicate filigree of aluminum mullions
screening a taut glass skin. At the building's core, however, is a solid box of concrete to protect the delicate artifacts with
high-tech climate control. ___ Taniguchi frames space vertically and horizontally, wrapping the building in successive
layers to get to its core—the Horyuji Treasures. The gallery really begins outside, beneath the towering triple-height
entry portico created by the overhanging roof, which is supported on delicate steel columns. To the left of this entry
facade is a narrower dining terrace sheltered by the same roof canopy, occupied by a restaurant operated by Tokyo's
famous Hotel Okura. Behind the glass entry facade is a triple-height lobby overlooking a reflecting pool and Ueno Park,
which turns the corner into the Okura's café. Sun pours in from skylights overhead, washing the lobby's limestone-
sheathed rear wall in daylight. ___ Behind the lobby, the ground floor contains exhibition galleries, including the spectacular display that is the heart of the building: a room of twenty-six miniature gilt-bronze Buddha statues mounted on
identical pedestals and encased in glass. The room is dark and moody, with strategically pointed spotlights illuminating
the grid of statues. Behind them is another dark, carefully lit gallery with other ancient treasures, including ritual dance
masks. The second floor contains a small, brightly lit reference and research area with a glass curtain-wall overlooking
the surrounding park, and the third level houses more gallery space and art storage. The top floor contains additional
storage and research areas, along with curatorial offices overlooking an unexpected internal courtyard at the center of
the floor plan. ___ Taniguchi's design contains elements of traditional Japanese architecture: asymmetrical compositions, a serene entry sequence surrounded by water and gardens, and thin screens separating indoor and outdoor space.
Of course, the architect rendered these traditional concepts in supremely modern forms and materials. His play
between architecture and nature is sublime: The broad reflecting pool at the museum's base reflects its diaphanous
facade, which in turn frames reflections of flowering cherry blossoms and the green copper cupolas of a neighboring neoclassical museum building. Taniguchi's Horyuji gallery is a discrete addition to Ueno Park, but far from a silent one.
___ Opposite: The Gallery of Horyuji Treasures is tucked into a corner of Ueno Park, behind the Beaux Arts
dome of the Tokyo National Museum.

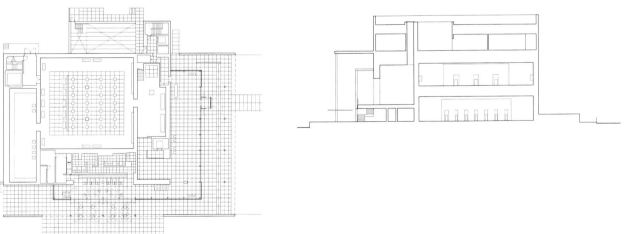

Above, from left: Ground-floor plan; section through galleries. —— Top: The gallery's main facade frames views of the surrounding park and captures reflections of neighboring buildings. —— Opposite, top: Thin mullions screen the upper reaches of the glass entry facade, overlooking a reflecting pool. —— Opposite, bottom left: A triple-height portico frames the entry facade. —— Opposite, bottom right: A long skylight above the double-height lobby washes the limestone-clad gallery wall in daylight.

Above: An additional display area is located outside the main gallery. —— Top: Sensitive artifacts are displayed within the concrete-framed gallery block, which is under careful environmental control. —— Opposite: A staircase leading from the lobby to the second-floor reference and research areas. —— Pages 20–21: The gallery's main attraction is a dramatic room with a grid of twenty-six gilded Buddhas displayed under glass.

Zurich architects Annette Gigon and Mike Guyer are known for cool, luminous structures that put a decidedly Modernist spin on alpine architecture, like the Kirchner Museum in Davos (1992) and an extension to the Kunstmuseum Wintherthur (1995), both in Switzerland. Gigon/Guyer's design for the

Liner Museum in rural Appenzell, Switzerland, is no exception. Built to house the portrait and landscape paintings of local father and son artists Carl Walter Liner and Carl August Liner, the 1,600-square-foot (17,200-square-foot) building is primarily a monographic museum. But it also accommodates changing exhibitions of contemporary art, as well as varying displays of the Liners's works. ___ The museum sits on the edge of Appenzell, between the rural hamlet and the surrounding alpine landscape. The exterior is covered in a simple but dramatic skin of large sandblasted stainless-steel panels, lapped like the shingles of the region's vernacular houses. There are a few large expanses of mullion-less glass that protrude from the steel-sheathed exterior; otherwise, the facades are predominantly solid. The building's energy comes from the play of light on its exterior—and from its jagged roofscape, created by a series of sawtooth gables that bring indirect light to the galleries below. The roof profile, which echoes both the repetitive skylights of old industrial buildings and the gabled roofs of traditional Appenzell houses, looks like a miniature mountain range within its alpine setting. ___ The architects have kept the gallery spaces neutral to allow flexible exhibitions to be mounted. The galleries themselves are quiet, contemplative spaces with poured concrete floors and simply detailed walls illuminated by daylight filtering through skylights in the gabled sawtooth roofs overhead. (The architects clad the angled roofs in the same sandblasted stainless steel as the exterior walls, to ensure that light reflected down into the galleries through the skylights would be as even and undistorted in color as possible.) Some galleries also have large expanses of glass that bring in additional daylight and open up the exhibition spaces to the dramatic landscape outside. ___ The museum's spacious vestibule and ticket lobby, which doubles as a meeting room and lecture hall, is the building's biggest interior room. From here, the gallery sequence unfolds as a series of rooms, diminishing in size as visitors move northward through the building. The architects kept the galleries relatively small to focus attention on individual paintings. The exhibition area is divided into ten galleries, each covering between 325 and 540 square feet (30 and 50 square meters) of space. ___ The central wall that separates the two rows of galleries remains fixed; the dividing walls perpendicular to it are placed at varying distances from each other to create gallery spaces of different sizes. The architects also varied the placement of openings in these dividing walls: Sometimes, the walls align axially; at other times, they are staggered. The net effect is a spatially varied experience for visitors. The architects also enlivened the sequence by breaking up the galleries at the halfway point with a small reading room and space for slide and video presentations at the north end of the building. Beyond its clarity and striking simplicity, the Liner Museum is innovative in its challenge to the numbing effect of so-called museum fatigue. ___ Below: Elevations showing the patterning of the shingled metal exteriors. ___ Opposite: A large mullion-less window punctuates the end of the gallery block.

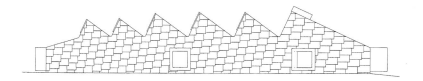 

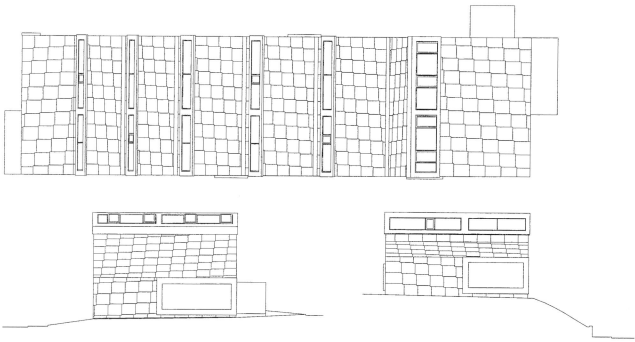

Above: Large sandblasted steel shingles, an abstract nod to traditional alpine architecture, create a silvery skin. —— Opposite, top: The building's sawtooth roofline gives it the appearance of an abstract mountain range. —— Opposite, bottom: Roof plan and elevations.

Above, left: A smaller window in one of the exhibition spaces breaks up the gallery sequence with light and views. ⎯⎯ Above, right: Gigon/Guyer varied the location of openings between galleries to create a more varied progression through the museum. ⎯⎯ Top: A large framed window opens the lobby to the surrounding landscape. ⎯⎯ Opposite: A close-up view of the gallery interior captures the building's strong, abstract quality.

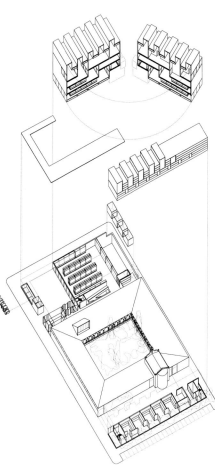

Madrid architects Luis Mansilla and Emilio Tuñón designed the Fine Arts Museum in the Valencian city of Castellón de la Plana as a delicate but hermetic vault for the city's historic treasures, including everything from Roman archaeological ruins to contemporary art. Founded in 1845, the regional

Mansilla + Tuñón	2001	
Museo de Bellas Artes Castellón		
Castellón de la Plana, Spain		

museum had many homes before moving into its present quarters: an old convent, a provincial hospital, and an eighteenth-century mansion, among others. Once again the museum is occupying historic quarters: the cloister of the former Serra Espada school. But this time, the historic structure has been woven together with a striking ensemble of muscular modern forms to create a strong contemporary presence for the institution. ___ The city sees the museum more as a comprehensive cultural center than as a pure museum. To wit, the program includes five permanent exhibition galleries, a temporary exhibition space, conservation and storage areas, offices, a library, an archive, an auditorium, a café, a classroom, and a conference facility. Mansilla + Tuñón's design comprises distinct but seamlessly conjoined structures to house the disparate program elements. The architects subsumed the old cloister, with its ancient cypress trees towering high above the open-air patio, between two entirely new wings. To the east of the cloister, a five-story block contains the museum's most public functions—that is, the galleries. To the west, a shorter volume houses restoration studios, workshops, and storage. A square ring behind the renovated cloister joins the two new structures and houses the library, an auditorium, a café, and the entry lobby, tucked into a corner of the square cloister. On one side of the shady cypress-filled courtyard is a wing of offices; on the other is a temporary exhibition gallery. ___ The exteriors of the new wings are clad in a taut skin that alternates solid and void, material and immaterial surfaces. Mansilla + Tuñón alternated opaque panels of recycled aluminum with a strong vertical crenelated profile with horizontal louvers, also made of aluminum. The bands of vertical and horizontal striations create an animated exterior that breaks down the building's large solid walls with an almost crosshatch texture. Light filters into the interiors through the louvered glass areas and through bands of milky translucent glass. The architects wrapped the spaces surrounding the patio with a similar skin of wood, glass, and masonry to match the exteriors of the new volumes. From the exterior, the only clue to the site's previous history is the grove of towering cypress trees extending out from the center of the complex. ___ Mansilla and Tuñón are alumni of Spanish architect Rafael Moneo's office, and their mastery of proportion and light—no doubt learned in Moneo's Madrid studio—is visible throughout the Castellón museum. The complex section that brings natural light and unexpected views diagonally through the five-story gallery wing is nothing short of spectacular. Light filters in from overhead skylights and towering clerestories and steps down through the building through double-height spaces linking smaller individual galleries. (The exhibits are divided into four broad categories: fine arts, archaeological treasures, ceramics, and crafts.) With its warm palette of rich wood and whitewashed walls and its masterly play of light, Mansilla + Tuñón's museum recalls Moneo's work and, in turn, the buildings of the Scandinavian legend Alvar Aalto, who greatly influenced Moneo. Mansilla + Tuñón created a simple, elegant backdrop for the Castellón region to celebrate its cultural history. Their architecture is strong but subtle, neutral but clearly visible. ___ Opposite, left: The new museum wing's recycled aluminum-clad box forms peer above the renovated cloister belonging to an old school. ___ Opposite, right: Exploded axonometric.

Above: Slender cypress trees towering above the cloister garden mark the center of the complex. ——
Opposite, top: A low-rise office wing separates the taller blocks containing galleries and restoration
areas. —— Opposite, bottom, from left: Plan; longitudinal section.

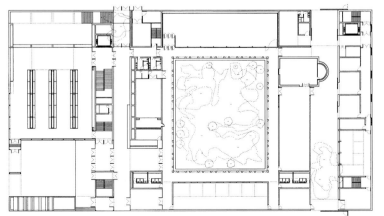

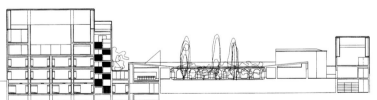

Above, left: Stacked double-height spaces create diagonal views through the gallery block, visible through large expanses of glass. ___ Above, right: Hanging pendant lamps echo the cascading profile of the galleries. ___ Opposite: The architects filter natural light through translucent glass and aluminum louvers over clear glass.

Above: The sectionally complex gallery wing creates views across exhibition spaces. The palette is a warm mix of natural materials bathed in daylight. ___ Opposite, top: Translucent panels bring daylight from multiple directions into the galleries. ___ Opposite, bottom: The ground-floor entry lobby, located in a corner of the former cloister, features an angular light monitor.

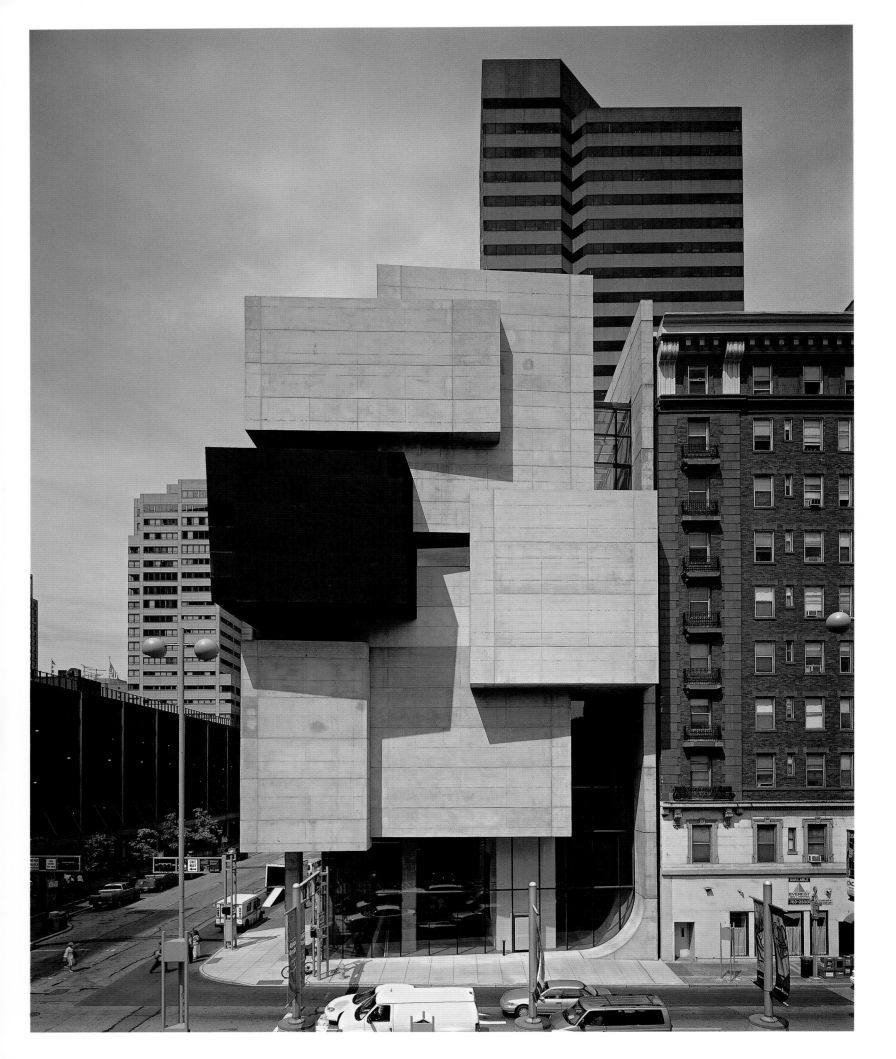

The Rosenthal Center for Contemporary Art is Pritzker Prize–winning architect Zaha Hadid's first building in the United States, and the first major American museum designed by a woman. It is also notable for its sophisticated interior spaces and the warm embrace of its urban environment—

Zaha Hadid Architects	2003	
Rosenthal Center for Contemporary Art		
Cincinnati, Ohio, USA		

all achieved for the relatively modest price of $20.5 million. ____ The center is not a collecting institution: It organizes and displays temporary exhibitions, installations, and performances. The institution had rented space in unceremonious locations throughout the city since its founding in 1939 as the Modern Art Society. Its new location on a prime corner in downtown Cincinnati—across the street from Cesar Pelli's Aronoff Center for the Arts—was a chance to increase its profile in the city. ____ Hadid wanted to draw the energy and activity of the city into the lobby and up into its galleries. To that end, she created an "urban carpet," a concrete floor that sweeps in from the sidewalk through the lobby and folds up like a skateboarding ramp to frame the backdrop of a dramatic atrium. The skylit atrium, extending the full six-story height of the building, features a kinetic, self-contained circulation spine. Ramplike stairs wrapped in steel box-beams energetically zigzag their way up through the skylit space to reach galleries on four floors. ____ Hadid's intent was to put everyone who uses the circulation spine in contact with all of the 87,500-square-foot (8,113-square-meter) building's functions. The ground floor contains the lobby, reception area, and museum shop; an underground level houses a black-box performance space. The third floor and part of the fourth are given over to the museum's offices and a staff lounge. The building's uppermost level contains a children's space, called the UnMuseum. The rest of the floors contain a variety of galleries—from double-height spaces to small and intimate rooms. ____ The exterior elevations reveal the building's interior organization. Hadid orchestrated volumes clad in precast concrete and anodized black aluminum into a dynamic massing of overlapping and intersecting blocks that stands out among Cincinnati's staid downtown buildings. On the south facade each floor level is clearly articulated with bands of precast concrete, glass, or anodized steel. The long, striated blocks align respectfully with the cornices and floor lines of an adjacent historic building. Hadid challenged the logic of gravity by placing blocks of steel and concrete above bands of glass. On the building's short side elevation, the exterior explodes with an energetic push-and-pull. The cantilevered ends of the individual volumes projecting beyond each other and over the street create a sculptural urban bas-relief. The upward thrust of the urban carpet is clearly visible as the concrete sidewalk moves into the ground-floor lobby and up against the adjoining building, extending up the full six stories. Hadid's building energizes the city, as well as the art within it. ____ Opposite: The Rosenthal Center's east-facing Walnut Street elevation is an energetic, abstract assembly of precast concrete and black anodized steel volumes cantilevering beyond each other. The volumes appear to float above the glass-enclosed lobby at street level.

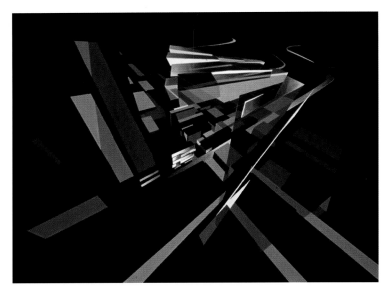

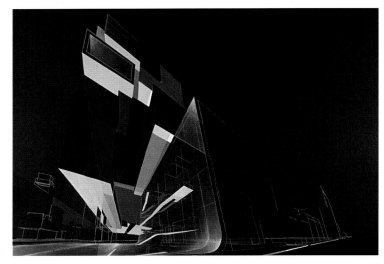

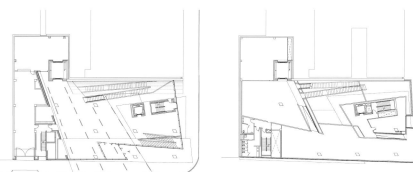

Above, drawings, from left: Entry-level plan; fifth-floor plan. —— Above: A conceptual model and paintings show Hadid's intent in creating an assemblage of floating volumes. The curving concrete plane of the "urban carpet" is visible in the center right rendering. —— Opposite: The building's long elevation appears as a more subdued composition of solid and glazed bars shifting subtly above the street.

Above: The fourth-floor gallery is a soaring, daylit space framed by the dramatic line of the steel stair-ramp angling up through the gallery. The hanging sculpture is Iñigo Manglano-Ovalle's *Cloud Prototype for an Edition of 3*. ___ Opposite, left, top and bottom: The museum features a variety of exhibition spaces, including this double-height gallery suitable for large-scale installations. ___ Opposite, right: Hadid brought the sidewalk into the double-height entry lobby and up into the museum with the "urban carpet," a concrete floor that curves up to become the back wall of the six-story space.

SKATEBOARDS,
BICYCLES, OR
CLIMBING NOT
PERMITTED
ON PREMISES

Above, from left: Longitudinal section; transverse section. ___ Top: The steel-encased stairs animate the skylit atrium. ___ Opposite: The building's "urban carpet" is so reminiscent of a skateboard ramp that museum authorities post signs prohibiting the activity.

It seems fitting that an architect who builds artful constructions from reinforced paper tubes would have been commissioned to design the Paper Art Museum in Shizuoka, Japan. Tokyo architect Shigeru Ban created such a museum for a paper manufacturer who wanted to showcase a collection

Shigeru Ban Architects	2002	
Paper Art Museum		
Shizuoka, Japan		

of contemporary art and Japanese graphic design and, of course, the art of making paper. Perhaps the only surprise of the commission is that Ban, who first used cardboard tubes to create an exhibition display in 1986, built the museum from more predictable materials. The museum joins an existing gallery previously renovated by Ban. ___ The 26,222-square-foot (2,437-square-meter) museum is made up of two separate volumes joined by a three-story atrium enclosed in clear glass balustrades that cantilever out into a void. The southern block contains three floors of offices; the northern wing provides exhibition space on two levels. Translucent bridges spanning the atrium join the disparate wings without interrupting the flow of daylight throughout the luminous atrium. ___ Although Ban eschewed cardboard for more orthodox building materials, the museum continues his penchant for technological experimentation. He skinned the building's steel frame in a double layer of Fiberglass Reinforced Plastic (FRP). On the south-facing garden elevation, hydraulic hinges lift the acrylic panels to completely open the facade to the elements while shading the interiors. When they are closed, the panels join to form a smooth translucent cladding. (Ban clad the final bays on either side of the hinged panels in the same FRP panels to create a continuous exterior when the panels are shut.) On the shorter east and west elevations, the exterior FRP panels slide to open up to the elements. The north facade is solid—and immovable. On this colder northern exposure, Ban used silica calcium boards that provide insulation as well as a solid surface for exhibition inside the gallery. ___ There is a continuing debate in the worlds of art and architecture over whether museums should be neutral containers completely subsidiary to the contents on display within them, works of art in their own right, or something between the two extremes. Ban's legacy of experimentation extends beyond materials and building techniques: He questions larger issues, such as blurring the boundaries between public and private space in a crowded contemporary city like Tokyo, as he did in his provocative Curtain Wall House of 1997, the unofficial poster child for the Museum of Modern Art's successful "Un-Private House" exhibition of 1999. ___ In this light, Ban's design for the Paper Art Museum is a challenge to the notion of the museum as a neutral container for art. Visually, the building is certainly neutral—as perhaps it should be, for displaying such delicate objects as paper and prints—but certainly not mute. Its movable panels, which create a fluid relationship between indoors and outdoors, energize the building with a kinetic energy that is unexpected for a little paper museum in central Japan, near Mt. Fuji. Once again, Ban challenges conventions to come up with a simple but provocative design that ultimately delights. ___ Opposite, top: The museum's garden elevation is skinned in a double-layer of translucent Fiberglass Reinforced Plastic (FRP). ___ Opposite, bottom: Hydraulic hinges lift the FRP skin to open up the facade to the exterior. ___ Page 46, drawings, from top: Exploded axonometric; ground-floor plan. ___ Page 46: The new structure's side elevation features a large central door in the translucent cladding that, when open, reveals a three-story atrium inside. ___ Page 47: Another structure features a wall of rolling doors that retract to reveal an exhibition space and create large awnings. ___ Page 48: The gallery opens onto a garden. ___ Page 49: In the new building, bridges span the central atrium, which is flanked by glass walls and crowned by a translucent roof.

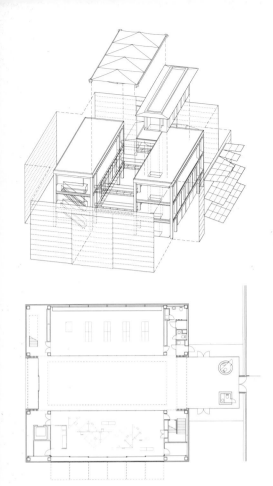

Architects Peter Cook and Colin Fournier describe their eye-popping design for the Kunsthaus Graz as a "friendly alien." The seeming dichotomy is apt: The bulging biomorphic building oozes through the city's staid urban fabric like a creature from another planet, yet it holds the edge of Graz's

Peter Cook and Colin Fournier	2002	
Kunsthaus Graz		
Graz, Austria		

streetscape like a good neighbor. And beneath the portly bulge of its blue-green fiberglass-skinned exhibition hall, crowned with skylights that look like ventricles protruding from a giant, sickly bodily organ, a ground level of floor-to-ceiling glass reflects the quaint pastel-colored eighteenth-century buildings of a charming city in the Austrian Alps. The curving upper level also reflects the surrounding context, creating an innovative visual dialog between old and new. ___ Cook was one of the founders of the pioneering British firm Archigram, which in the 1960s challenged architectural conventions with bold utopian designs for "walking cities" and other visionary theoretical projects. Four decades later, Cook and Fournier, working with two German firms in a joint venture called ARGE Kunsthaus, have succeeded in giving form to Archigram's iconoclastic vision. And this avant-garde vision has helped transform a run-down section of the city with what has proven to be a popular new building: Cafés and restaurants have sprung up around the Kunsthaus. ___ The Kunsthaus covers 118,360 square feet (11,000 square meters) over several levels, both above and below ground level. Because it is not a collecting institution, the museum was designed with an eye toward maximum flexibility. The curving exterior houses two levels of black-box exhibition spaces that can be adapted to display contemporary art, photography, or other media. An exposed bridge connects Cook and Fournier's undulating exhibition halls with an adjoining historic cast-iron building dating from the 1850s. ___ The high-tech skin covering the upper levels of the Kunsthaus is composed of a grid of tinted acrylic glass panels clipped in place at each corner. The exterior conceals a double-layer construction: Beneath the outermost layer of acrylic glass tiles are 925 standard circular fluorescent tubes. Thanks to an innovative computer-controlled system, the lights can be modulated to create a range of intensities, allowing the curving facade to not only glow, but also to become a giant low-resolution screen for displaying messages, gray-scale animation, and film clips. ___ Inside, the bubbling outer skin defines open flexible exhibition spaces. The nozzle-shaped light scoops that poke out from the exterior like anatomical ventricles bring natural light into the galleries; electronically controlled louvers limit the amount of daylight allowed into the space. Directly beneath the light scoops, set into hexagonal openings in the faceted, paneled ceiling, are coil-shaped fluorescent tubes that supplement the natural light in the gallery. Like the rest of the building, these funky light fixtures have a familiar yet unfamiliar look to them—cool-glowing hotplates hovering above a vast interior defined by an alien skin. ___ For all its formal quirkiness, the exhibition pavilion is a hospitable addition to Graz—adding flexible gallery space to the city's center and energizing its context. In the end, the building is not so alien after all. ___ Opposite: The "friendly alien" stands out from its neighbors with a bulbous electronic skin and round skylights.

Below, from top: Floor plan; section. —— Opposite: The building's translucent acrylic skin conceals a grid of circular fluorescent tubes that animate the facade.

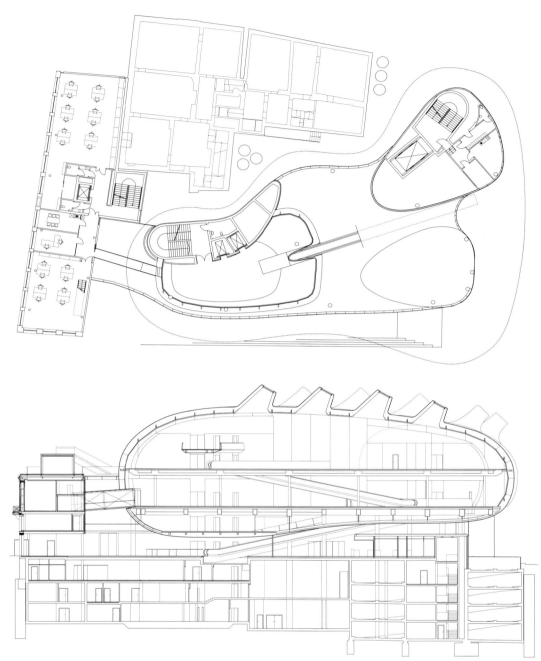

Above: The building's curvaceous profile winds its way through Graz's historic cityscape. ___ Opposite, top: The skin is covered in a grid of clipped acrylic panels. ___ Opposite, bottom: Circular skylights extend from the main body of the building like anatomical vessels. ___ Page 56: Circular fluorescent tubes integrated into the facade create a changing pattern of electronic messages and animation. ___ Page 57, top: Large open gallery spaces allow for flexible exhibitions. ___ Page 57, bottom: Some areas feature corkscrew fixtures beneath skylights that are visible from outside.

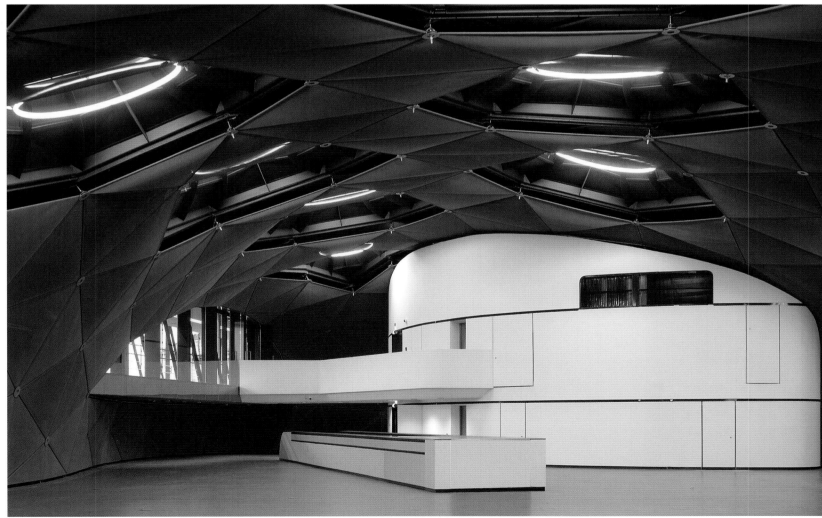

Tadao Ando's Modern Art Museum of Fort Worth (MAM) sits across the street from one of the most famous museums of the twentieth century: Louis I. Kahn's sublime Kimbell Art Museum, opened in 1972. More precisely, the parking lot of Ando's museum sits across the street from Kahn's Kimbell;

Tadao Ando Architect & Associates	2002	
Modern Art Museum of Fort Worth		
Fort Worth, Texas, USA		

the museum itself is off to one side, avoiding a direct comparison between two of the greatest modern architects, both of whom worked wonders in concrete. In the new MAM, the only visible nods to Kahn's famous vaults are long gallery pavilions that extend from a huge reflecting pond on the east side to a sculpture terrace on the west. Otherwise, Ando created his own unique world animated by plays of light and water in the Texas city's cultural district. ___ The new building is more than four times the size of the museum's previous home, with 53,000 square feet (4,926 square meters) of gallery space alone. The overall museum contains 153,000 square feet (14,221 square meters) of space on two levels. The entrance from the parking lot—the main point of entry in car-dominated Texas—leads into a double-height entry lobby filled with natural light. To the right, within the short end of the L-shaped floor plan, are an auditorium, a café/restaurant with an outdoor terrace, and a suite of offices; to the left are more offices, the museum shop, and a suite of galleries, which fill out the long leg of the L. The loading dock, storage, and art preparation areas are located behind the galleries. Upstairs, the floor plan is the same as on the ground floor, with the addition of classrooms at the south end of the gallery wing and a sculpture terrace above the storage and loading dock. The overall plan frames a shallow gravel-bottomed pond that creates a reflective pedestal for the entire building. ___ The galleries themselves are as much about providing areas for exhibiting large-scale works of art as they are about presenting the dramatic spaces that terminate each of the parallel pavilions with brightly sunlit halls overlooking the reflecting pond. These areas give visitors a visual and spatial break from the art, preventing so-called museum fatigue; they also let visitors take in Ando's intertwined play of concrete, glass, light, and water. Daylight fills many of the galleries, but it is carefully filtered and screened through skylights and louvers in order to avoid damaging artworks. ___ Ando's signature material is concrete, and he usually renders it with exactly crafted precision. The concrete in the Fort Worth museum is no less spectacular—even though, unlike the Kimbell Museum, the MAM is a concrete building contained within a lightweight shell of glass. During the daytime, the only major evidence of concrete on the building's exterior is the wishbone-shaped columns supporting flat slab roofs above the glass-enclosed gallery pavilions that jut out into a pool of water on the east side of the museum. At night, when the pavilions glow like giant lanterns, the concrete walls bathed in light are visible from the outside. That illuminated vision gets to the essence of Ando's elegant design. ___ Below: Sections. ___ Opposite: Richard Serra's *Vortex* anchors a corner of Tadao Ando's museum building.

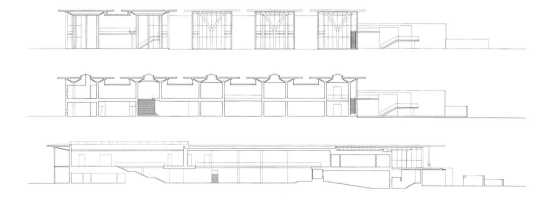

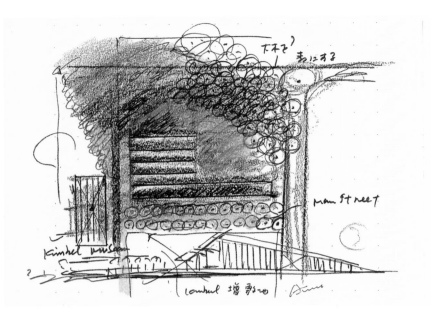

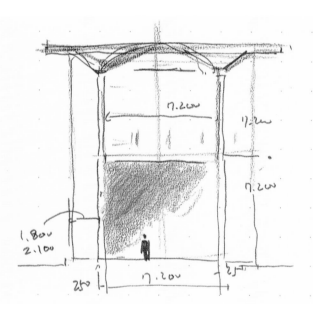

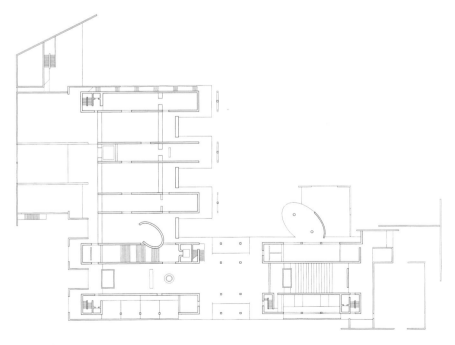

Above: The building's glass-enclosed pavilions seem to spring from a reflecting pool defined by the L-shaped structure. ___ Opposite, top: One of Ando's sketches for the museum site, which is adjacent to Louis Kahn's Kimbell Art Museum. ___ Opposite, center: Ando's sketch for one of the new museum's bays. ___ Opposite, bottom: Floor plan.

Above: Nightfall changes the appearance of the museum, opening up views to the solid cores inside the galleries. ___ Opposite: Walls of floor-to-ceiling glass open the interior to views of the cityscape beyond the reflecting pool.

Above: The vaulted concrete interior of Ando's building pays homage to Louis Kahn's neighboring Kimbell Art Museum. ____ Opposite, top: The galleries have varying heights and lighting sources. ____ Opposite, bottom: In the lobby, Ando's pristine concrete walls are washed in natural light from both sides.

Sir Norman Foster's renovation of the grand courtyard that was buried, literally, at the heart of the venerable British Museum is simultaneously and somewhat paradoxically a simple renovation and an extreme makeover. Foster's design is simple for its extreme clarity: spanning the courtyard

Foster and Partners	2000
Great Court, British Museum	
London, UK	

with the weblike lattice of an enormous curving skylight that wraps the freestanding Reading Room at the center of the court. But the project is extreme in its transformation of an open-air courtyard—filled with a hodgepodge of structures housing the British Library's book stacks and kept off-limits to everyone but scholars—into a grand enclosed space that gives coherence to one of the world's great museums. ___ Foster's Queen Elizabeth II Great Court, which was dedicated in December 2000, was made possible by the decampment of the library from within the confines of the British Museum, originally designed by Sir Robert Smirke, to a new building in Saint Pancras in 1996. Once the stacks were cleared, Foster could begin work on the deceptively simple—but technically complex—building process. The project involved a number of separate but related jobs: restoring three of the Ionic limestone porticoes framing the quadrangle and reconstructing the missing south portico, which had been destroyed during an expansion in 1875; building a new subterranean structure to house an education center; and restoring the cast-iron dome and the delicate painted interiors of the Reading Room. Simultaneously, Foster covered the courtyard with the vast but visually delicate skylight that spans the cylindrical drum of the Reading Room and the four facades of the courtyard. The skylight undulates vertically and spirals outward horizontally to negotiate the difficult geometry of the building, appearing to float effortlessly above the courtyard—even though it weighs 1,000 tons. Foster also wrapped the newly exposed Reading Room in pale Spanish limestone to match the surrounding facades. ___ While the Great Court is now a grand public space, there are new spaces for museum-related functions seamlessly integrated into Foster's design. Visitors enter the space through the entrance hall fronted by an outdoor court on Great Russell Street in the literary enclave of Bloomsbury. Facing the limestone-covered Reading Room, two broad staircases wrap the sides of the drum-shaped structure to reach a gallery on the second floor and a restaurant on the third level, where a glass bridge leads to galleries in the north wing of the original building. The restaurant and gallery are contained within an elliptical addition that hugs the north side of the Reading Room; on the ground floor, that ellipse makes room for a gift shop tucked discretely from the street entrance. ___ Foster's dramatic transformation of the Great Court is just the first phase in a multistage project that will eventually create new galleries, restore historic interiors, and add a study center within the walls of the original Smirke building, where the Rosetta Stone and Elgin Marbles continue to draw throngs of visitors. The serene courtyard now fills the heart of the museum with light and air, while giving a sense of order and clarity to a once confusing museum experience. ___ Opposite: The curving latticelike skylight above the Great Court springs from the refurbished courtyard facades.

Below, from top: Section of museum complex showing Reading Room; diagram of skylight structure; floor plan. ____ Opposite: The curvaceous skylight wraps the circular drum of the domed Reading Room at the center of the Great Court.

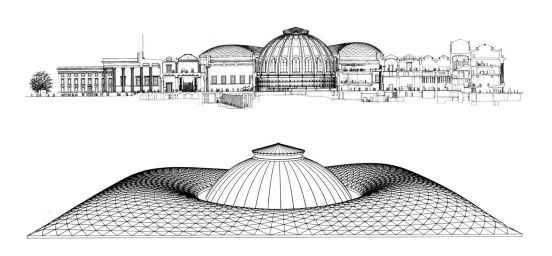

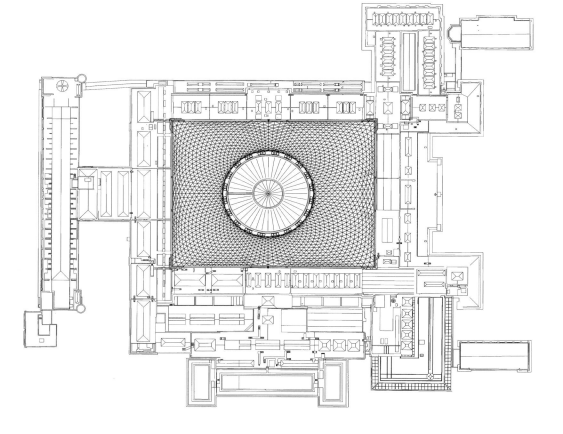

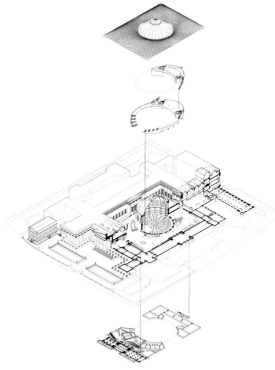

Above: The vast skylight floods the Great Court with daylight, creating a protected "outdoor" lobby at the heart of the British Museum. —— Opposite, top: New staircases wind around the newly stone-clad reading room, leading up to new visitor services on the second level. —— Opposite, bottom: Exploded axonometric.

Pritzker Prize–winning Swiss architects Jacques Herzog and Pierre de Meuron were commissioned by the Emannuel Hoffman Foundation—which was founded in 1933 and counts works by Salvador Dalí, Paul Klee, and more than 150 other artists among its collection—to design a combi-

Herzog & de Meuron	2003
Schaulager	
Basel, Switzerland	

nation warehouse, exhibition space, and research center in Basel. The foundation had exhibited its works at the Basel Museum of Art and the Museum of Contemporary Art, but needed a space to both store and exhibit its holdings. Herzog & de Meuron responded by creating the Schaulager, or Viewing Warehouse, a climatically controlled box that accommodates the disparate needs of art storage and art exhibition. The architects were unaware of any existing building type to which they could look for inspiration, but were "fascinated and challenged" by the problem and began the design process by engaging in a rigorous debate with their clients. ___ Herzog & de Meuron initially considered condensing all of the art into a single large space without any dividing walls. All of the collection's works would be displayed cheek-by-jowl like a "junk-shop," as the architects lightheartedly suggested, with the added benefit of being able to survey the foundation's entire collection at once within the vast storage and display area. But curatorial concerns about the proper conservation and transport of works led the architects in a different direction. They decided that creating a space that was primarily a warehouse—and celebrated as such, with floor-by-floor storage and stacking expressed architecturally—was the way to go, offering the curators both flexibility and proper technical accommodations. ___ From the exterior, the Schaulager is a dramatic four-story sculptural box covered in an unusual textured concrete. The concrete was mixed with aggregate excavated from the site, to give the building a physical connection to its context, as if the building had been extruded from the ground or exposed like an archaeological dig. The entry facade is cut away to create a huge, sheltered forecourt or portico with a small gatehouse flanked by a pair of LED screens that display art pieces commissioned by the foundation. The gabled form of the gatehouse makes it look like an artistic installation—an abstraction of an alpine hut rendered in the same concrete mix as the main building. Along one side of the building, an undulating ribbonlike incision in the concrete reinforces the excavated quality of the exterior, although this profile was created with digital technology. ___ Inside, a towering atrium creates a dramatic welcome and reveals the five floors in a single glance. The lower two floors contain gallery space for temporary exhibitions as well as permanent installations by artists Robert Gober and Katharina Fritsch. These 19.7-foot-tall (6-meter-tall) galleries can be freely partitioned according to the exhibition on view. The upper three floors are given over to storage spaces custom-designed for the Hoffman Foundation's collection. The Schaulager's storage spaces cover roughly 78,000 square feet (7,250 square meters), almost half the building's total area. The building also contains administrative offices, art handling areas, workshops, and a 144-seat auditorium that resembles an excavated cave or grotto. ___ The Schaulager raises provocative questions about the distinctions between the display of art and the behind-the-scenes workings necessary to bring art to the public eye. Storage, preparation, handling, and conservation areas consume huge amounts of square footage, yet they usually remain invisible to visitors. Herzog & de Meuron's thinking was, why not condense these two separate and distinct domains into one? The result is an energetic, efficient new kind of building that changes our views of both the warehouse and the museum. With this design, Herzog & de Meuron have re-engineered two different typologies—and possibly have created an entirely new one. ___ **Opposite: Herzog & de Meuron designed the Schaulager—a combination warehouse, exhibition space, and research center—as a climatically controlled sculptural box. A soaring canopy shelters the indented entry, which is flanked by a pair of large LED screens.**

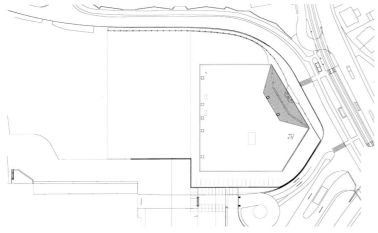

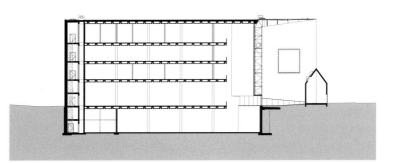

Above, from left: Site plan; section with entry canopy. ____ Top left: Beneath the entry canopy is a small, abstract guardhouse containing the entrance to the building. ____ Top right: The interior of the guardhouse is spare: exposed concrete lit by round skylights. ____ Opposite: The exteriors of the four-story building are covered in concrete made with aggregate excavated from the site. ____ Page 76: Ribbonlike windows cut into the concrete exterior to reveal glazing behind. ____ Page 77, top: The jagged profile of the concrete outside the windows suggests a random act, but the incisions were guided by digital technology. ____ Page 77, bottom: Floor plans. ____ Page 78, top: The molded interiors have a cloudlike, confectionary appearance. ____ Page 78, bottom: The auditorium resembles an excavated cave or grotto. ____ Page 79: The soaring atrium reveals the repetitive floor plates and lighting plans of the museum-cum-storage facility.

In his now iconic Jewish Museum in Berlin (page 120), Daniel Libeskind demonstrated the kind of dark, moody power his twisted, fragmented forms could evoke in visitors. Libeskind's design itself proved enough to strike strong emotions in museumgoers who visited the empty building before even a single artifact was placed. In the Imperial War Museum North, the architect of the Ground Zero master plan in Manhattan tried to evoke similarly strong responses about war and peace as he did about the Holocaust in Berlin. ___ Located on the Salford Quays of Manchester, England, the museum is an outpost of the London-based Imperial War Museum, which also operates a branch in Duxford, England, that houses vintage aircraft in a sleek hangar designed by Sir Norman Foster. The Manchester location displays warplanes and cannons; it also puts on an impressive high-tech video show, with images from its vast historical archives projected on the walls of the galleries. ___ The building covers 69,940 square feet (6,500 square meters) on two levels. The lower level contains the lobby—reached by passing through the "air shard," an empty, angled tower nearly 95 feet (30 meters) tall crisscrossed by a cage of tubular steel struts—as well as a gift shop, offices, and classrooms. The upper level houses the double-height permanent and temporary exhibition spaces, along with a restaurant. Visitors can take an elevator up the air shard to reach a viewing platform with vistas of the once-vibrant industrial port of Manchester, heavily bombed during World War II. ___ The canted shard is one of three fragmented volumes representing segments of a shattered sphere that comprise the museum's exterior. The exhibition spaces are sheltered beneath the largest of the three shards, a convex form that contrasts with the smaller volume housing the restaurant and other functions, which fits beneath a concave wedge that tapers up to a point. Each of the three masses is clad in metal panels with different finishes and textures—some gridded, others ribbed. ___ Libeskind's typically aggressive language of sharp angles and violent slashes is felt throughout the museum: walls containing punched-out openings filled with strip lights strike a disjointed geometry with the walls and columns around them. Beams of light projected onto the angular walls of the exhibition areas also seem to slash through space. Limited views to the exterior make the museum a highly internalized experience: The only connections to the exterior are narrow, slotted skylights that slice through the vaulted metal roof. ___ The floor of the galleries has a slight concavity to it, creating a subtle but perceptible sensation of being off-balance. Indeed, it is Libeskind's intent to always keep the visitor on guard and off balance. As in the Jewish Museum in Berlin, the architecture offers an experience that goes well beyond the artifacts. ___ Below: Elevations. ___ Opposite: The museum's exterior is composed of three fragmented volumes that suggest a shattered globe.

Studio Daniel Libeskind	2002
Imperial War Museum North	
Manchester, UK	

Above: The 95-foot-tall (30-meter-tall) "air shard" dominates the museum's exterior. ⎯⎯ Opposite, top left: A shallow convex curve shelters the exhibition volume. ⎯⎯ Opposite, top right: The "air shard" is an empty tower crisscrossed by an exposed steel structure. ⎯⎯ Opposite, bottom left: Libeskind's stark forms suggest a violent crash. ⎯⎯ Opposite, bottom right: Part of the exterior is clad in a gridded metal skin.

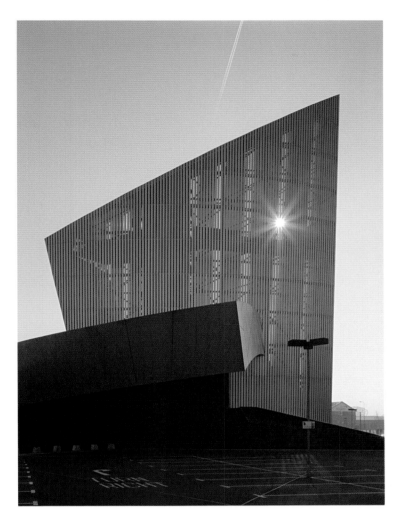

Above, left: A broad metal curve defines the two-story exhibition wing. —— Above, right: Visitors enter the museum through the base of the "air shard." —— Opposite: An interior staircase conveys the architect's intent to create an unbalancing sensation.

Above: Gallery walls follow the building's overall geometry. ___ Opposite, top left: In the exhibition spaces, lighting concealed in angular strips echoes the building's fragmented forms. ___ Opposite, top right: Clashing geometries are also visible in the café. ___ Opposite, bottom: Floor plan.

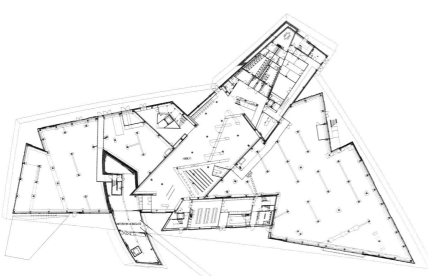

The O Museum, dedicated to traditional Japanese painting, is perched on a wooded mountainside in Nagano Prefecture in north-central Japan. Architects Kazuyo Sejima and Ryue Nishizawa of the innovative Tokyo firm SANAA designed the museum as a simple glass structure that would—to borrow

Kazuyo Sejima + Ryue Nishizawa/SANAA	1999
O Museum	
Nagano, Japan	

a line from the master Australian Modernist and Pritzker Prize laureate Glenn Murcutt—touch the earth lightly, both physically and visually. In typical SANAA fashion, the result is sublime. Sejima and Nishizawa created a gossamer glass bar that undulates gently along its 266-foot (80-meter) length, creating sexy, subtle plays of surface and skin as it winds above the hillside. ___ To protect the archives and delicate objects on display from humidity, the architects raised the slinky glass box off the site on six steel columns wrapped in glass. That freed up the ground plane for the purely pragmatic element of the design—most notably toilets, which are housed in a cylindrical drum abutting a small spiral staircase that provides secondary access to and egress from the long exhibition space on the first floor. This move allowed the entire first floor to remain a single free and clear space. ___ The main entry to the museum is along a ramp extending up the back side of the structure. The front side overlooks the ruins of an ancient Japanese building, separated from the museum structure by a narrow gravel-covered courtyard. The facade overlooking the historic structure remnants appears to be a uniform skin of taut glass extending from the visually thin floor to the equally thin roof. The skin is actually composed of rectangular panels joined together with a tiny square clip at each corner. Except for a large rectangular patch of clear glass that frames a view of the castle from inside the lobby, the surface is uniformly patterned with thin white lines etched into the glazed wall. Behind the glass, however, the interior surfaces change several times along the length of the structure, becoming opaque or translucent depending on the fragility of the objects on display inside. On the back facade, the architects simply rendered the skin completely opaque as needed. ___ This change between transparency and opacity is even more pronounced inside the museum. Standing at the far end of the space and looking toward the opposite end, the interior appears to telescope in and out as areas change from translucent to opaque. The lobby, for instance, features black floors and ceilings and translucent walls marked by etched line patterning. Further down the structure, separated by glass walls and doors, a gallery space is finished with white floors and ceilings and enclosed by thick opaque white walls on opposite sides. The effect is that of a subtle, sophisticated fun house for art. ___ Sejima and Nishizawa's design is, like most of SANAA's work, simple and richly nuanced. With minimal means, the museum creates a space entirely at the service of art, yet one that engages its surroundings physically and visually. It not only preserves the best features of the woodland setting, but also enriches the site with its presence. ___ Opposite: The O Museum's undulating etched-glass skin floats above the ground. Glass-encased columns lift the steel-framed structure a full story above grade to protect the museum's delicate artifacts from humidity.

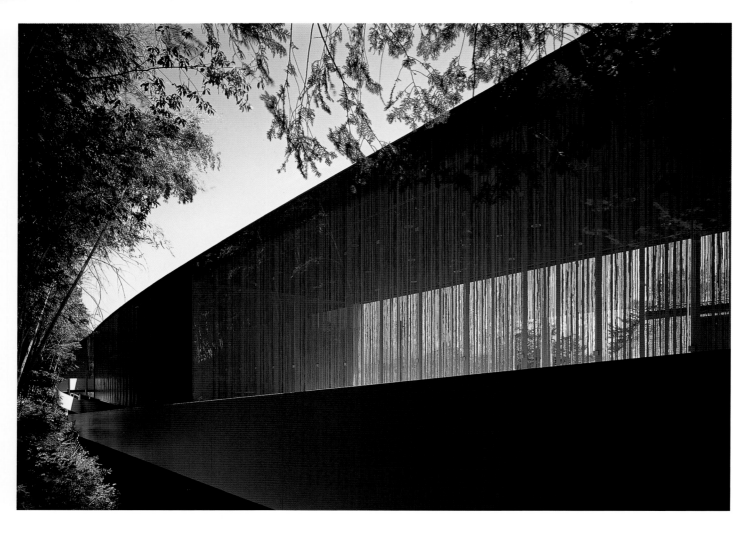

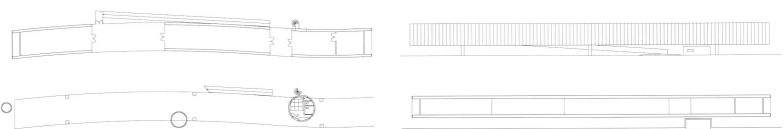

Above, clockwise from top left: First-floor plan; elevation; longitudinal section; ground-floor plan. ___ Top: The interior is a single volume that curves gently down its length. Changes in the floor-to-ceiling glass skin—from opaque to veiled with an etched pattern of thin lines to transparent—create a variety of visual effects in a small structure. ___ Opposite, top: A ramp rising along the back side of the museum structure leads to the entrance. ___ Opposite, bottom: The architects kept portions of the exterior skin opaque, to protect sensitive objects from damaging daylight. ___ Pages 92–93: Looking out from the lobby space, the adjoining remains of a historical building are framed by a swath of clear glass in the etched facade.

There is no mistaking the function behind the Vulcania Museum in St. Ours-les-Roches, France, created by the Viennese architect Hans Hollein. From a distance, the split conical form of the museum rises above the flat landscape of the Massif Central—part of an extinct volcano—

Hans Hollein	2002
Vulcania Museum	
St. Ours-Les-Roches, France	

and resembles nothing so much as an abstract volcano itself. The project, devoted to the history of volcanoes in southwestern Europe, is the brainchild of former French president Valéry Giscard d'Estaing, now the provincial governor of the Auvergne region where the museum is located. Giscard d'Estaing's intent for the museum was to boost tourism to this area of France. ___ The volcano-like cone is just one part of the sprawling 195,832 square-foot (18,200-square-meter) European Center of Vulcanology, the core of which is a museum documenting the effects of volcanic activity on the earth. Its signature form is composed of two partial cones, measuring up to 92 feet (28 meters) in height, that overlap each other; a truss bridge slips between the segments, linking the lobby, two large amphitheaters, and temporary exhibition space inside to a more traditional wing with a restaurant on its top floor. The nested cone segments are clad in dark panels of volcanic basalt stone on the outside; the exposed interior surface is finished in a texturally animated skin of golden vapor-treated steel panels that reflect sunlight, creating a bright counterpoint to the dark, solid exterior. The golden lining suggests the contrast between the solid exterior and explosive, lava-filled interiors of actual volcanoes. ___ Most of the Vulcania Museum is located, appropriately, below ground. From the towering cone, visitors descend along a winding ramp into a large artificial crater ringed by walls of black basalt stone. The ramp leads down to a patch of volcanic rocks at the center of the 125-foot-deep (38-meter-deep) man-made crater, part of an old lava flow on the site. Small balconies around the perimeter of the large void offer visitors spots from which to look down at the stones at the core. Like Hollein's literal evocation of a volcano above ground, the path along the crater's walls quite clearly suggests a voyage to the center of the earth. Another linear path winds past the remnants of a second lava flow. ___ The other functions of the museum are built into the landscape and organized radially around the sunken clearing dominated by the cone-towers. A large greenhouse structure, crowned with a vaulted glass roof, displays towering ferns and other local flora of the Auvergne region in a volcanic landscape. The giant greenhouse overlooks an ancient lava flow, now stone. A large auditorium at ground level shows 3-D films about the geological history of the Massif Central region. The rest of the museum's display areas, given over to documentaries of famous eruptions from Pompeii to Mount St. Helen's and other exhibitions, are all located underground. ___ Hollein's design for Vulcania resembles his notable Abteiburg Museum in Mönchengladbach, Germany, of 1982, which was built into its site and clad in a mixed palette of stone. At Vulcania, the cladding—some surfaces covered in honed blocks of basalt, others rough hefts of volcanic stone—comes out of the earth from which the building is excavated, creating a strong link between architecture and site. Even though the conical towers have a strong outward appearance, Hollein's building plays a secondary role to the site. It's an aggressive design that still strikes a delicate balance with its landscape. ___ Opposite: The Vulcania Museum's distinguishing element is a large conical form rising from the flat landscape, which is part of an extinct volcano.

Above: The interior of the fractured cone is finished in a reflective pattern of gold-colored stainless steel. ___ Opposite, top: A curving wall of volcanic stone frames a ramp leading down from ground level to a preserved lava flow. ___ Opposite, bottom left: A bridge extending out from the large volcano-like cone leads to the rest of the museum complex. ___ Opposite, bottom right: The interior of the towering cone contrasts with the black volcanic basalt stone cladding its exterior.

Above: A segmented ceiling continues the radial geometry of the site plan. —— Top left: An enclosed pavilion offers a glimpse of an old lava flow beneath ground level. —— Top right: A large vaulted greenhouse shelters a volcanic garden exhibit. —— Center left: A large auditorium is housed in a separate structure. —— Opposite, top: A ramp winds down to a preserved lava flow deep within the site, with platforms from which to view the rock formation. —— Opposite, bottom, from left: Site plan; axonometric.

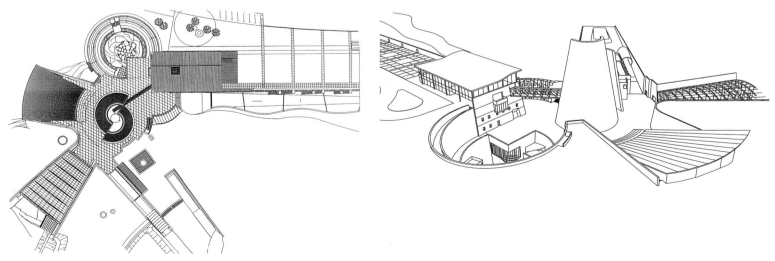

The architect Roger Diener—who joined his father Marcus's firm in the 1970s and now runs offices in Basel and Berlin bearing both their names—is a hyper-rationalist architect in the vein of O.M. Ungers and other Swiss and German Modernists. In Biel, near his Basel office, Diener designed

Diener & Diener Architekten	1999
Centre PasquArt	
Biel, Switzerland	

a building for the Centre PasquArt, a private contemporary art foundation established in 1991 with a collection of approximately 1,200 works by mostly Swiss artists. Among its holdings, the PasquArt foundation counts an important collection of works by the Swiss artist Bruno Meier and bequeathals of engravings by H.P. Kohler from Biel and Martin Ziegelmüller of Belgium. ___ Previously, Diener has been called upon to add spare, simple wings onto more elaborate historical structures. For an addition to the Swiss embassy in Berlin (2001), the architect added a minimalist concrete box to a similarly square-lined neoclassical pavilion. On the front facade, Diener abstracted the original embassy's classical tripartite facade with spare window openings placed asymmetrically; on the side elevation, the pattern of window openings takes on its own rhythm and language—a grid of six windows wide by four windows tall. ___ At the Centre PasquArt, Diener's approach to adding onto history was even more spartan. Since 1990, the center has made its home in a pair of historic buildings in the quiet hamlet of Biel. The main structure was built in 1886 as Biel's first hospital; the building was expanded in 1955 with a west wing that functioned as an old-age home. Ten years after setting up shop in these repurposed buildings, the Centre PasquArt moved into its expanded facility, with Diener's competition-winning design for a wing at the eastern end of the ensemble of buildings. The architect was also responsible for renovating the historic structures to create a unified, updated art venue. ___ Diener makes no pretense that his addition is somehow a continuation of the existing buildings: With its stark stone facade, fairly nonexistent articulation, and sympathetic but distinct geometry, the building clearly delineates what is old and what is new. The latest wing attaches itself to the back of the main 1886 building but keeps a respectful distance along the main facade, where a narrow gap distinguishes the two (as if the sudden change in materials and language were not enough to make that point clear). Diener's wing also stops short of the height of the existing structure: three stories instead of the original four. ___ The ground-floor entry space is completely glazed to allow views of the surrounding mountains. A simple band of floor-to-ceiling glass in thick dark frames is recessed from the floors above. The second level is divided into three longitudinal galleries, as indicated on the facade by three simple mullion-less windows that abstractly echo the tall rectangular proportions of the original building's windows. The top floor contains a dramatic open exhibition hall crowned by six rows of skylights embedded in the 19-foot-tall (5.8-meter-tall) space. This 3,927-square-foot (365-square-meter) gallery is a blank canvas for artists who can take advantage of its soaring ceiling height and generous daylight. Diener's restrained approach lets art—and history—stake out its own ground in this young institutional setting. ___ Opposite: Diener & Diener added a new stone-clad wing onto a former hospital building occupied by the Centre PasquArt. The entry level of the new structure is set back from upper floors and features floor-to-ceiling glass to open up views of the surrounding mountains.

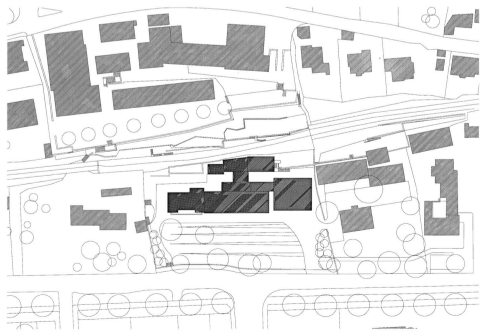

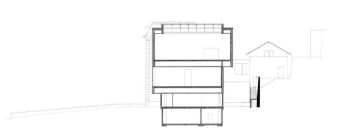

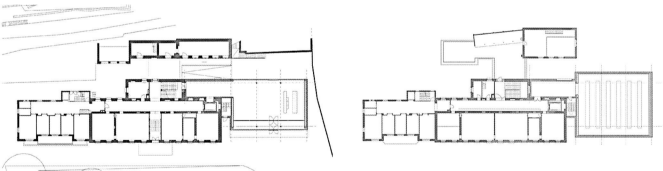

Above, from left: Ground-floor plan; top-floor plan. ⎯ Top: The new addition, with dark stone and spare window openings, clearly sets itself apart from the historic original. ⎯ Opposite, top: An overhead view of the addition's form within the scenic backdrop of hillside treetops and neighboring buildings. ⎯ Opposite, bottom, from left: Site plan; section. ⎯ Page 104, top: Thick-framed glass doors enclose the entry lobby. ⎯ Page 104, bottom: The light-filled lobby is surrounded by glass walls and doors. ⎯ Page 105, top: Second-floor galleries are arranged behind full-height windows on the front facade. ⎯ Page 105, bottom: Other galleries connect to the outdoors with large mullion-less windows.

Palmach, an underground Jewish organization that fought against British rule in the former Palestine, was incorporated into the Israeli army after the nation was established in 1948. In 1992, a Palmach veterans' group that included the former Israeli prime minister Yitzhak

Rabin held an architectural competition to design a museum commemorating the history of this once clandestine faction and its role in the creation of the Israeli state. The winner of that competition was Zvi Hecker, a Polish-born architect based in Tel Aviv and Berlin. ___ To say that Hecker's museum integrates itself into the landscape would be an understatement. Seen from across the road, the structure resembles a series of rough stone terraces interspersed with angular concrete planes rising to opposite ends of the site—or perhaps a ruin, or an ancient geological formation shored up by concrete walls. Indeed, Hecker describes the entire museum as "essentially a landscape." (He tempers the physical description, however, with the allegory of "a landscape of the dreams that have made Israel a reality.") In fact, the stone walls, clad in rough but thin kurkar sandstone salvaged from the excavation work on the site, are the creation of Hecker and partner Rafi Segal. The only thing original to the site is a rocky outcropping of earth and a cluster of trees that the architects preserved within a central courtyard. They built the rest of the 54,868-square-foot (5,100-square-meter) museum around this salvaged patch of landscape, the only soft spot in a tough building that redefines Brutalism with a regionalist edge. ___ One enters the museum at the bottom-most level, and continues up a ramp that moves from street level in an early clue to the building's deep, almost geological relationship with the site. The entrance foyer is two-thirds of the way up the ramp. From here one moves either into the temporary exhibition area or down another ramp to reach the museum itself, which rings the courtyard below ground level. The museum contains artifacts from the Israeli war of independence and a memorial to Palmach. The installations are comprised of a multimedia mix of exhibitions, including a scale version of Tel Aviv's Herzl Street in 1941, vintage newsreel footage of World War II, and a film tracing the training of fictional Palmach recruits. ___ Beyond the museum block, the building opens up into a complex composition of angular volumes finished in rough kurkar stone and exposed poured-in-place concrete panels. At one end of the courtyard, adjoining the bare-concrete auditorium block (with seating for 400), is an outdoor amphitheater with curving concrete steps. Here, visitors watch a film projected against exposed concrete walls. A large opening in the exterior walls frames views of the surrounding landscape. The remainder of the site is taken up by a café and a memorial to the slain Yitzhak Rabin; beneath them is an underground parking structure. On the back side of the building, away from the street, the concrete has been left unfinished—the museum is awaiting future additions—but the rough, unpolished surfaces don't seem out of place on such a rugged building. The concrete seems part of the tough, complex play of volumes in Hecker's design. ___ Opposite: Hecker used kurkar limestone salvaged from the earth during construction to clad a large heft of the building; the stone contrasts with poured-in-place concrete elements. ___ Page 108, top: From the street, the Palmach Museum appears to be built into an excavated cliff; the rough kurkar limestone that was unearthed during construction now clads a new aboveground structure. ___ Page 108, bottom: The limestone-clad wing frames a concrete ramp leading up to the entrance.

Above: An angular opening in the concrete wall overlooking the city creates a framed view next to the open-air theater. ___ Opposite, top left: A shaded window is set into a towering stone wall. ___ Opposite, top right: Some of the museum's concrete surfaces are left unfinished, awaiting future additions. ___ Opposite, bottom, from left: Floor plan; site plan. ___ Page 109, top: Curving concrete platforms create an open-air amphitheater with framed views through an opening in the concrete wall. ___ Page 109, bottom: Concrete and stone volumes are interwoven with natural landscape elements.

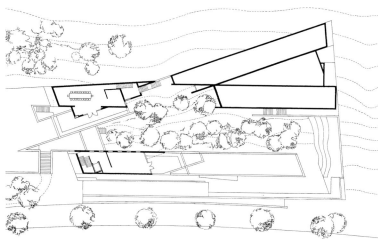

Above: The exhibition wing overlooks a tree-filled central courtyard. —— Opposite, top: A staircase in the exhibition area ends in a glass-enclosed space overlooking the central courtyard. —— Opposite, bottom: Windows in the lowest level of galleries overlook the street.

The tree-lined stretch of West 53rd Street in Manhattan between Fifth and Sixth Avenues is something of a cultural corridor. Besides the newly enlarged Museum of Modern Art, which dominates the block, the street is also home to the Museum of Art and Design (formerly the American Craft

Tod Williams Billie Tsien & Associates	2001
American Folk Art Museum	
New York, New York, USA	

Museum), and the American Folk Art Museum, designed by New York architects Tod Williams and Billie Tsien. When it opened in 2001, the Folk Art Museum marked the first time that a new museum had been built from the ground up in New York City since Marcel Breuer's imposing Whitney Museum of American Art opened its doors in 1966. The Williams + Tsien building may also be one of the city's smallest museums. Although its footprint measures just 40 feet wide by 100 feet deep (12 meters by 30 meters), the museum's design stakes out a strong physical presence. ___ The scale of the six-story building (there are also two subterranean levels) is diminutive, but Williams + Tsien played up its intimacy and almost residential scale to create a "house for folk art," as they call it. Indeed, the museum's trustees were drawn to the architects' work in particular because of a townhouse they had designed for an art collector in New York; the designers took the analogy of a townhouse as a jumping-off point for their design. ___ Visitors walk into the museum through an off-center entrance in the striking facade, a folded composition clad in panels of tombasil, a white bronze alloy typically used to craft boat propellers and other prosaic objects. The architects cast the metal panels against the rough concrete floor of a foundry in Beacon, New York, which imbues them with a mysterious, bubbly texture. ___ To one side of the narrow lobby is the gift shop; at the rear is a double-height, skylit atrium that leads to a sculptural staircase at the northwest corner of the building. One level up is a mezzanine overlooking the atrium and a café with windows facing Eero Saarinen's landmark CBS Building across the street; the two subterranean levels contain offices, a library, a classroom, and an auditorium. The second through fifth floors contain gallery spaces arranged around a narrow atrium at the center of the building, which is penetrated by a wide staircase. There is also a third staircase: a narrow run of steps that hugs the east wall of the building, connecting the fourth- and fifth-floor galleries. ___ Besides the tombasil exterior, the museum contains the subtle, sophisticated play of materials for which Williams + Tsien are well known. Polished wood contrasts with warm pietra piasentina stone and concrete, hammered and sandblasted to expose its rough aggregate. Luminous green panels of cast fiberglass frame the main staircase. Such warm materials and highly crafted details are appropriate for a museum of rustic folk art and a welcome departure from the typical museum of neutral boxes. ___ Below: Sketches for the subtly folded facade, which the architects liken to a mask. ___ Opposite: The museum's entry facade, made of cast panels of a bronze alloy, makes a suitable backdrop for a vest-pocket park next to Eero Saarinen's CBS Building (in foreground).

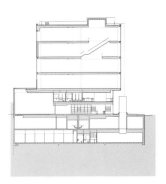 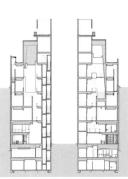 

Above, from left: Longitudinal section; transverse section; sectional axonometric. ___ Top left: Drips and bubbles give the tombasil panels that make up the faceted exterior a strong tactile quality. ___ Top right: A translucent skylight poking aboveground, next to the museum's shop, brings light down to two subterranean levels. ___ Opposite: A narrow skylit atrium brings daylight down to the entry foyer.

Above: At the back of the ground floor, a skylit atrium filled with highlights of the museum's collection of folk art objects starts the sequence up to the galleries via a concrete stair. —— Opposite, top left: Panels of luminous green fiberglass, clipped to the concrete staircase behind, appear to float away from the stairs. —— Opposite, top and center right: Hammered, sandblasted concrete contrasts with the rich warm wood of a built-in bench and a handrail on a glass partition. —— Opposite, bottom, from left: Floor plans of the first to sixth floors.

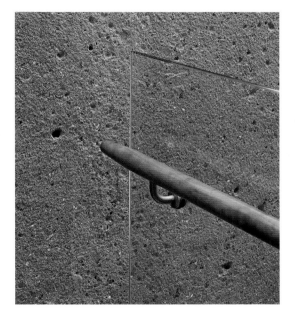
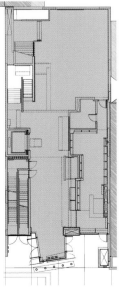
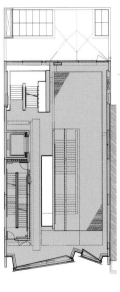
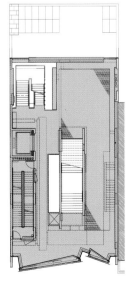
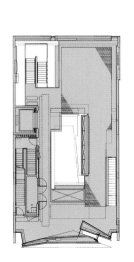
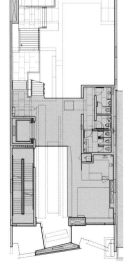
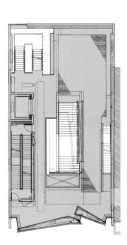

Daniel Libeskind became a household name when he was chosen in 2003 to create the master plan for the redevelopment of the World Trade Center site in downtown New York. The building that truly put him on the international architecture map, however, was his 1989 competition-

Studio Daniel Libeskind	1998
Jewish Museum Berlin	
Berlin, Germany	

winning scheme for the Jewish Museum in Berlin. Libeskind's design is so powerful as an artifact in its own right that the museum was unveiled in 1999 with nothing in it. Even empty, the building could evoke the sense of loss and dislocation inflicted on Europe's Jewish population by World War II and the Holocaust. ___ The museum, which finally opened in 2001, is located on Lindenstrasse next to a classical red tile-roofed building in central Berlin. Libeskind sets the stage for the building's narrative of disruption and dislocation by breaking Lindenstrasse's regular edge. The plan zigzags away from the street like an unfurled angular ribbon. Libeskind conceptualized the building as the jagged lines of a fractured three-dimensional Star of David slicing deep into the site. The museum's main presence along the street is a void dominated by the striking ETA Hoffmann Garden. This truly disorienting spatial feature is a large sunken square set into a lawn in front of the museum building. Visitors descend into the excavated concrete basin that defines the space and wander among the forty-nine concrete shafts projecting in a grid from the base of the garden. These towering shafts, skewed at a sharp angle, terminate in precariously planted trees. The feeling of uneasiness and disorientation is palpable as one wanders through the gridded forest of concrete shafts and distant trees—precisely Libeskind's intention. ___ Behind the garden, the museum unfolds as jagged, slender four-story volumes clad in narrow bands of zinc. The exposed vertical seams between the zinc panels give the largely opaque facades a sense of rhythm and scale. Parts of the metal skin are scored with thin incisions that, like the building's plan, suggest the geometry of an exploded Star of David. The pattern of openings changes around the museum's perimeter: In some places it reveals large expanses of windows beneath; in others it creates the thinnest of openings, some shaped like dashes and crosses. Exposed rivets beneath some of these slotted windows give the building a tough, foreboding character. The violent scores in the facades make themselves felt inside the narrow galleries, which unfold through the museum along a circuitous route that Libeskind calls *die Leere*, or "the emptiness." ___ Libeskind's distinct formal language has often been imitated; but in his Jewish Museum, it derives from a unique reading of the building's program and its urban site. More importantly, Libeskind developed this language in Berlin to create a particular emotional effect on the visitor—and it works exceedingly well. The general sensation of emptiness and uneasiness—not the desired effect of most buildings—is palpable. The immense popularity of the museum is proof of Libeskind's success in meeting the stated goals of his design. The building is the museum's most important artifact. ___ Opposite: Slashes in the museum's metal skin echo the building's jagged plan. ___ Page 122, top: A focal point of the museum is the ETA Hoffmann Garden, a grid of canted concrete shafts planted with trees. ___ Page 122, bottom: Visitors descend into the angled concrete base of the Hoffmann garden to experience a disorienting, disquieting sensation. ___ Page 123, top: The museum building, with a plan based on a deconstructed Star of David, unfolds around the concrete monument, away from the street. ___ Page 123, bottom: Sections.

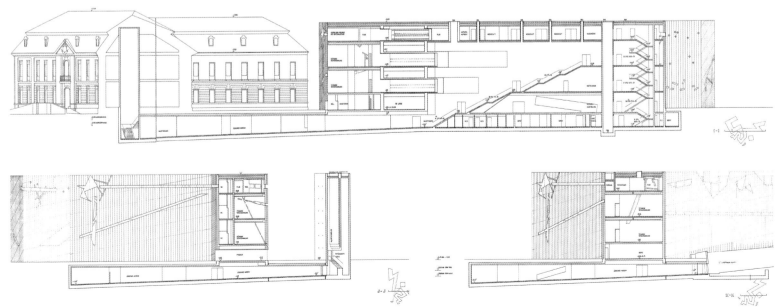

Above, left: The zigzag pattern of window openings along the main Lindenstrasse facade reveals the exploded Star of David motif of the plan. ___ Above, right: The cut-away segments of the exterior, sometimes edged with exposed rivets, have a tough, industrial aesthetic. ___ Opposite: Narrow gashes in the exterior contrast with the patterning of the metal panels. ___ Page 126, top: Given the tracery of angular slotted windows, light tracks in the ceiling, and intersecting walls, the gallery spaces have a strong identity, even when empty. ___ Page 126, bottom: Cutouts in the exterior skin reveal the secondary geometry of the exposed window frames beneath. ___ Page 127, top: Gallery spaces offer a complex play between light and dark, solid and void. ___ Page 127, bottom: Plans of the museum depict the design's zigzagging discontinuity.

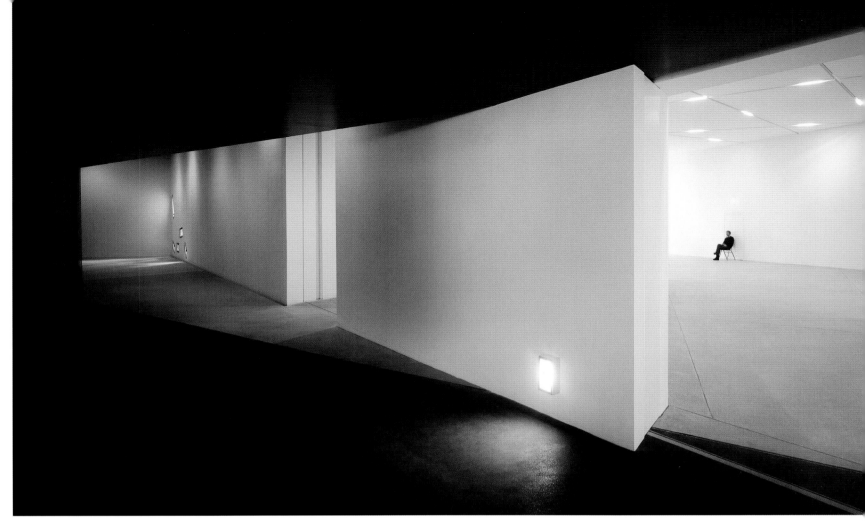

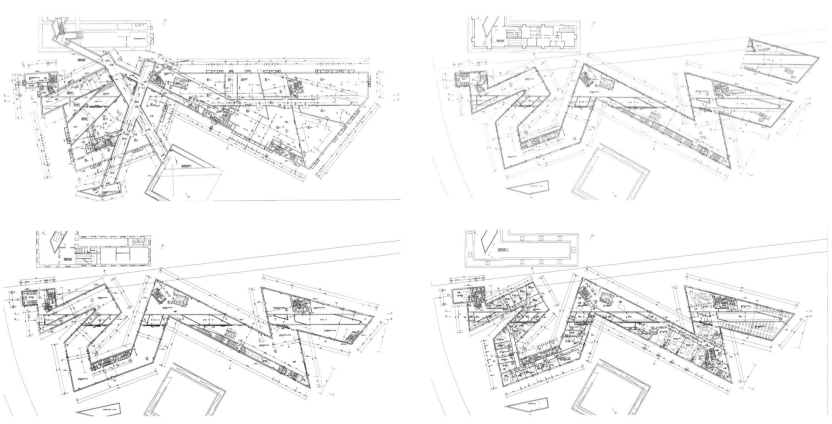

The city of Vienna is a vast museum filled with centuries' worth of exquisite architectural and urbanistic treasures. The MuseumsQuartier Wien is a sprawling cultural complex within the grand city, housed both in repurposed baroque buildings that once served as the Imperial stables and in

Ortner & Ortner	2001
Museum of Modern Art Ludwig Foundation	
Vienna, Austria	

new purpose-built structures. The architecture firm of Ortner & Ortner, based in Berlin and Vienna, designed the sprawling complex, including three new structures: the Leopold Museum, the Kunsthalle Wien (attached to a preserved stable building), and the Museum of Modern Art Ludwig Foundation. These structures are set behind the complex of institutions housed in the long expanse of former stable buildings, and include media production studios, an architecture center, a children's museum, and a collection of smaller dance, media, performance, and other arts groups known as quartier21. In total, the quarter contains more than 600,000 square feet (55,770 square meters) of exhibition space. Its planners tout the vast complex as "baroque meets cyberspace." ___ One of the centerpieces of the MuseumsQuartier is Ortner & Ortner's design for the Ludwig Foundation. Known by its German acronym MUMOK, the foundation is Austria's largest museum for modern and contemporary art. The museum's stark profile—a taut, vaulted black box covered in volcanic black basalt stone—creates a counterpoint to the Leopold Museum (dedicated to Austrian Modernism, including the world's largest collection of works by Egon Schiele), a slightly larger white box, clad in white limestone. Separating the two is the Kunsthalle, with its restored stable building fronting a new brick-clad addition at the rear. ___ The Ludwig Museum contains 51,640 square feet (4,800 square meters) of exhibition space spread over four floors: two levels above the entrance, which is 13 feet (4 meters) above the level of the surrounding plaza, and two levels below the entry. (As in the Leopold Museum, a broad external staircase connects the plaza with the elevated foyer level.) The top-floor galleries take on the ceiling profile of the building's gently vaulted roof, which is pierced with bands of arched skylights. Slicing though the full height of the building is a dramatic skylit atrium that cleaves a deep luminous chasm through the stone-clad cube. The building's circulation wraps around this towering space, bringing visitors in touch with daylight in a building that has few windows onto the outside world. ___ On the exterior, Ortner & Ortner clad the simple, straightforward volume in a 4.7-inch-thick (12-centimeter-thick) wrapper of volcanic black basalt stone. The architects varied the width and thickness of the stone panels to create a subtly rich and textured exterior with a single material; they also peppered the facade with an irregular pattern of narrow slot windows. Far from mute, the exterior hums with a quiet kinetic energy. Aside from its strong, simple shape among so many elaborate baroque buildings, the museum's stark blackness is its signature element. The building reveals subtle shifts of light and shadow, and its playful texture invites discovery as one moves around it. In the end, it's a neutral container for an important collection of art, but it's not a passive player in the richly complex urban landscape of Vienna. ___ Opposite: Architects Ortner & Ortner inserted the white cube of the Leopold Museum, at left, and the black cube of the Ludwig Foundation museum, at right, behind the long Baroque buildings of Vienna's former Imperial stables. The stables and new buildings now house the various cultural institutions that comprise the MuseumsQuartier.

Above: The Ludwig Foundation's monochromatic exterior is animated only by subtle shifts in the basalt cladding and narrow slit windows between the stone blocks. ____ Opposite, top: The architects clad the vaulted Ludwig Foundation building in a shell of volcanic black basalt stone. ____ Opposite, bottom: The Leopold Museum is a compact box, clad in white limestone.

Above: A broad flight of stairs between the Ludwig Foundation building and the renovated baroque shell of the Kunsthalle leads to the foundation's elevated entrance. A similar broad exterior staircase leads to the entrance of the limestone-clad Leopold Museum. ____ Opposite, clockwise from top left: Elevations; longitudinal section; transverse section.

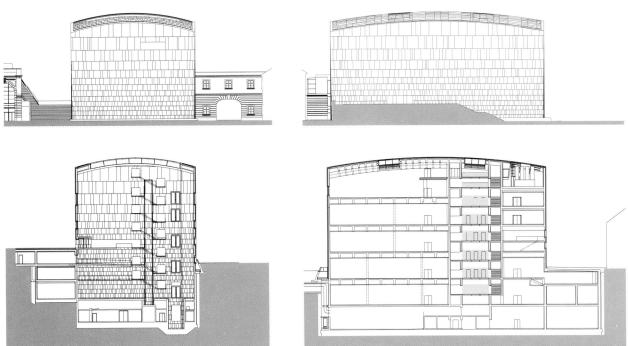

Above, left: A dramatic skylit circulation atrium slices through the height of the Ludwig Foundation museum. —— Above, right: Another atmospherically lit circulation space. —— Opposite, top: A vaulted skylit gallery crowns the top floor of the Ludwig Foundation building. —— Opposite, bottom: A similar vaulted gallery is located in a new addition to the historic winter riding stable, now the Kunsthalle.

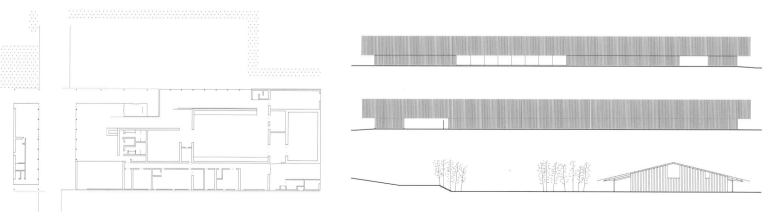

The Japanese artist Hiroshige Ando (1797–1858) is regarded as an important figure in the *ukiyo-e*, or popular, style of wood-block landscape prints. When the town of Bato in Tochigi prefecture (about three hours from Tokyo) received a rare gift of ink drawings on paper done by Ando and

Kengo Kuma & Associates	2000
Museum of Hiroshige Ando	
Bato, Japan	

decided to create a new museum to house them, Japanese architect Kengo Kuma received the commission. ___ Kuma took inspiration with the way Ando depicted landscapes under the altering effects of wind, rain, and fog in his works. Kuma, a master of manipulating views through subtle screens, used delicate cedar poles to define the museum's slatted walls and roofs. The strategy owes a large debt to Ando's famous work *Rain on Travelers*, in which the artist portrays rain falling on people crossing a bridge with a pattern of thin lines. By varying the spacing between the timber rods, Kuma was able to create a variety of levels of transparency, consequently altering views between the rods. ___ Although the effect Kuma created was complex, the museum's design is quite simple: a long rectangular bar with a crisp shed roof dominating a spare entry court covered in dark gravel. (Beneath the delicate exterior cladding is a sturdy steel-frame structure.) The approach to the museum is along a stark stone path within the gravel courtyard, a long, low opening in the exterior wall that is framed by rows of towering bamboo on either side of the entryway. To the right of the large portal is a shop and café; to the left are the galleries. ___ Two types of timber screens shade windows that extend the length of the entry facade: the deep overhang of the slatted roof on the outside and a scrim of cedar posts just inside the glass. The slatted facades modulate the daylight coming into the museum as well as the views of nature from the galleries. At night, the whole of the long facade glows softly when illuminated from within. ___ Throughout the large, open interior, Kuma defined internal rooms with varying densities of timber scrims on the ceilings and walls. When lit from within, these internal rooms look like glowing patches of rain, as if Ando's famous work had come to life. Interior corridors are defined by thin walls of handmade paper, which are backlit to create an even glow of light. At the core of the building are dark, dimly lit galleries where Ando's delicate works are exhibited far from the damaging rays of natural light. Other gallery spaces display the work of local artists. ___ Like the "floating worlds" depicted in *ukiyo-e* prints, Kuma's crisp but sensuous design seems ethereal, like a glowing apparition hovering mysteriously in a clearing in the unremarkable surroundings of Bato. Though Kuma rendered his strikingly simple structure in natural materials, the building does not read as a natural thing, but rather as an extremely controlled composition that happens to be made from thin strips of wood. What matters most is the sublime effect of Kuma's design. It bows to Ando's work with a studied neutrality, yet stakes out its own aesthetic territory. ___ Opposite, top: The wooden slats enclosing the museum screen out the building's surroundings. ___ Opposite, bottom, clockwise from left: Plans; front elevation; back elevation; side elevation. ___ Page 138: At night, the building's long glass walls are illuminated from within to reveal translucent paper walls inside. ___ Page 139, top and bottom: The slatted roof extends beyond the confines of an otherwise simple shed structure.

Above: Interior spaces are defined by slatted timber screens—which recall the painter Ando's striated lines that suggest rain—and translucent and solid walls. —— Opposite: Looking back toward the entrance, the café is visible beyond the open entry court. —— Page 140: The thin battens, which create a delicate shadow on the ground, are reflected in the museum's long glazed entry facade. Ando's work can be seen within the gallery on rolling display cases. —— Page 141, top: The wood ceiling battens filter light from above. —— Page 141, bottom: Along part of the entry facade, the glazed skin is set back from the exterior to create a breezy indoor-outdoor space.

The Genoese architect Renzo Piano is known internationally for delicate, exceedingly well-crafted museums that place the necessities of art above the whims of architecture. His design for the $70 million Nasher Sculpture Center in Dallas is no exception. Like his Menil Collection and Cy Twombly Gallery

Renzo Piano Building Workshop | **2003**

Nasher Sculpture Center

Dallas, Texas, USA

in nearby Houston, Piano's 55,000-square-foot (5,110 square-meter) Nasher Center is material yet immaterial, a minimal museum with great visual impact. —— The gallery and sculpture garden occupy 2.4 acres in downtown Dallas's Arts District, across from the Museum of Art by Edward Larrabee Barnes and a block from I.M. Pei's Meyerson Symphony Center. Local collector and philanthropist Raymond Nasher asked Piano for a museum without a roof, to give maximum daylight for viewing his extensive collection of nineteenth- and twentieth-century sculptures by Rodin, Giacometti, Brancusi, Richard Serra, and Mark DiSuvero. Piano designed a series of five conjoined pavilions with glass barrel-vaulted roofs. The pavilions measure 112 feet (34 meters) long and 32 feet (10 meters) wide. Thin walls of travertine separate the pavilions; floor-to-ceiling glass curtain walls at either end open the vaulted spaces to the exterior. —— The barrel vaults that crown the gallery pavilions are made of glass with a low iron content that keeps the glazing as clear as possible, thus creating optimal light conditions for viewing the richly textured sculptures below. The glass vaults are supported from below by narrow steel ribs and from above by delicate stainless-steel cables. To cut down on direct sunlight and over-powering shadows, Piano added perforated aluminum sunscreens above the curved glass roof. He hid all of the sophisticated infrastructure, including cabling and ventilation ducts, within the thin travertine walls, and integrated artificial lighting within the overhead structure, to keep the space as clean and free of visual clutter as possible. —— Three of the five contiguous vaults contain sculpture galleries; the remaining two are given over to a shop, a café, and a boardroom. An underground level contains galleries for light-sensitive artworks, research facilities, a conservation lab, an auditorium, and offices. The palette throughout the interiors is purposefully simple, to keep the emphasis on the art contained within: white oak floors, polished travertine walls, and the aluminum and extra-clear glass of the vaulted roofs. —— The adjacent 1.5-acre garden, the work of landscape architect Peter Walker, is an integral part of Piano's design. This oasis of green among the skyscrapers of downtown Dallas provides exhibition space for the Nasher Center's largest works, as well as additional breathing room around the gallery building. Rotating selections of sculptures from the collection are displayed among native Texan trees, including live oaks, cedar elms, magnolias, and weeping willows, as well as pools and fountains. Also in the garden are dozens of works by Polish artist Magdalena Abakanowicz, a Picasso, and James Turrell's *Tending (Blue)*, a "skyscape" created by the light artist specifically for the garden. —— Below: Site plan. —— Opposite: The Nasher Sculpture Center is composed of five long, conjoined vaulted spaces. The adjacent garden, designed by landscape architect Peter Walker, covers most of the 2.4-acre site and includes rows of native trees and a site-specific James Turrell installation.

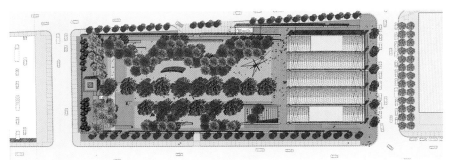

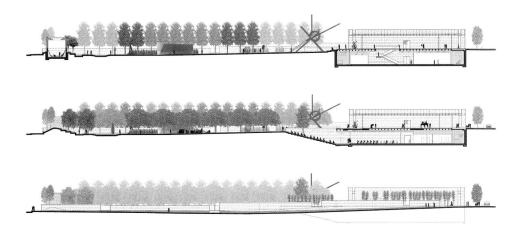

Above: Sections through the galleries and sculpture garden. ____ Opposite: The conjoined pavilions, separated by thin walls of travertine, measure 32 feet (10 meters) wide. Floor-to-ceiling glass curtain walls at either end open the vaulted spaces to the exterior.

Above: The galleries are simple vaulted spaces with hardwood floors and travertine walls. ___ Opposite: The glass vaults above the gallery feature low-iron glazing to make them as clear as possible, which makes for better viewing of art objects.

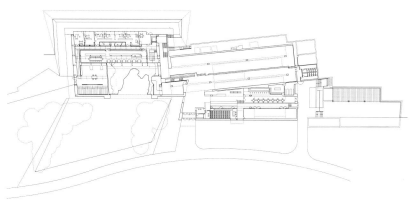

The architect Juan Navarro Baldeweg has kept a relatively low profile despite having designed several exquisite museum buildings in his native Spain. Also an accomplished painter, Baldeweg displays a keen sensitivity to light and space. His most recent commission is a new museum at the site of

the famous Altamira caves in northern Spain, where Paleolithic-era cave paintings thought to be among the oldest human works of art were discovered in the nineteenth century. The UNESCO-protected caves were open to the public for much of the early twentieth century, but were declared off-limits in 1979 after scientists realized that the huge crowds were causing damage to the bright red paintings of bison hunts and other prehistoric rituals. The new museum includes reproductions of the sensitive cave paintings and displays of Stone Age artifacts, as well as a scientific research complex, a library, and administrative offices for the institution charged with maintaining the original caves. Baldeweg's design combines the simulated cave and research center into a single hillside structure near the original Altamira site. ___ As one might expect, Baldeweg took advantage of the sloping site to create a building that, appropriately, buries itself at least partially into the earth. From the exterior it is difficult to discern that there is in fact a building on the rural landscape of Cantabria, a northern region between Galicia and the Pyrenees that happens to be the Madrid-based Baldeweg's native province. Thick walls clad in local ashlar stone define stepped grass-covered terraces punctuated by a series of long light monitors. A pergola connecting the building with a parking garage is one of the few overtly architectural elements suggesting an actual building on the site. ___ The linear 60,000-square-foot (5,574-square-meter) complex is divided roughly into three contiguous segments. One zone contains administrative offices and a library; another, the artificial cave, reached by a series of ramps; and the third houses the entry hall, permanent and temporary exhibition spaces, multipurpose rooms, a book store, and a café. ___ Baldeweg carefully re-created the conditions of the actual Altamira cave in his tourist-friendly facsimile, copying the cave and its opening down to the most minute physical details. More importantly, however, he measured the amount of daylight that reached the ceiling surface of the original, so that viewers in his re-creation could view the paintings under similar lighting conditions. (A single opening at the top of the simulated cave keeps visitors in touch with the outside world, even in the depths of the cavern.) This is Baldeweg at his art-world best. ___ The architect's painterly side is evident in the bright colors that mark the few architectural elements visible above ground. Baldeweg does not use color as gratuitous appliqué; rather, he chooses natural materials that will communicate a particular hue, and uses applied color only sparingly. At Altamira, the bright green of the grass-covered terraces, the thick stone's natural pale-pink tones, and the blue-green of the glass create a palette as strong as the ochre and flat red the architect chose for colored surfaces. This play of natural and artificial color is like the museum itself, a provocative interplay of the natural and the manmade, between architecture and landscape. ___ Opposite, top: The museum is composed of low-slung sheds set into the hillside site. ___ Opposite, bottom: Site plan.

Above: The museum is composed of long skylit volumes that step down with the surrounding topography. —— Top: Colors like ochre mark the cultural complex's few overtly architectural elements. —— Opposite, top: A wooden pergola leads to a parking area. —— Opposite, bottom: The architect designed an exact replica of the historically important Altamira Cave, with ramps descending into the artificial cavern. He carefully imitated the natural light under which simulations of the original Paleolithic paintings can be viewed. —— Page 154: The roof of the artificial cave is suspended from a series of tensile cables beneath a skylit ceiling. —— Page 155, top: Baldeweg, himself a painter, is keenly sensitive to illuminating art, as is indicated in this linear gallery beneath a canted ceiling plane. —— Page 155, bottom: A series of long clerestories bounce daylight into the space.

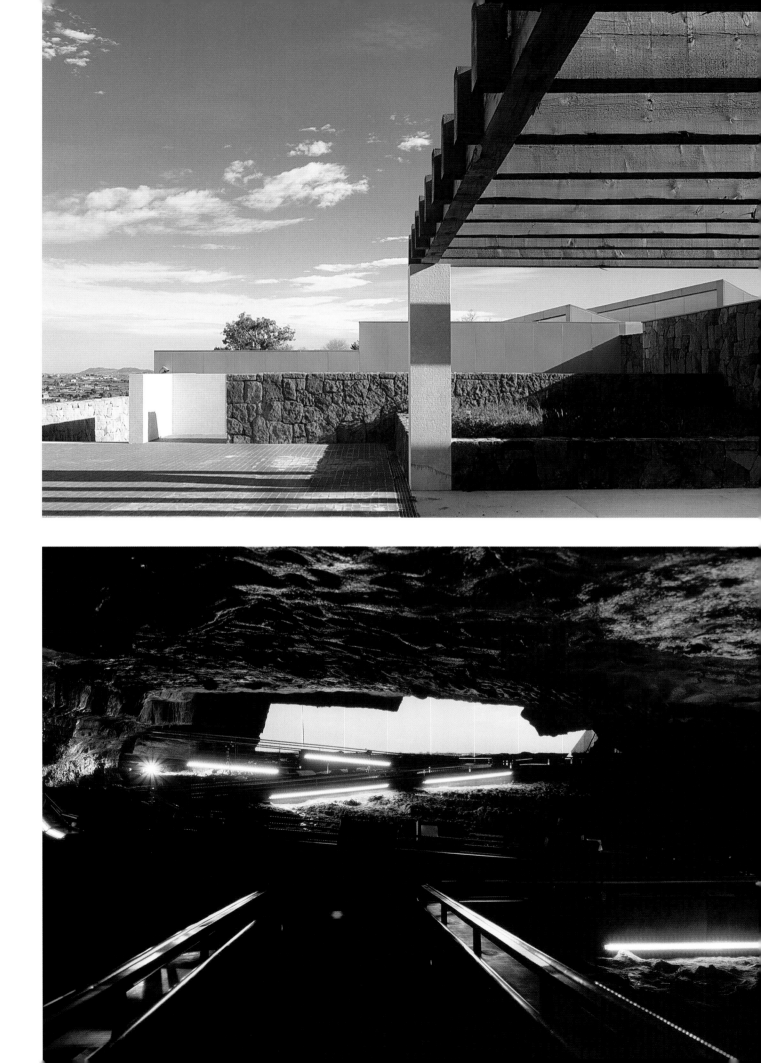

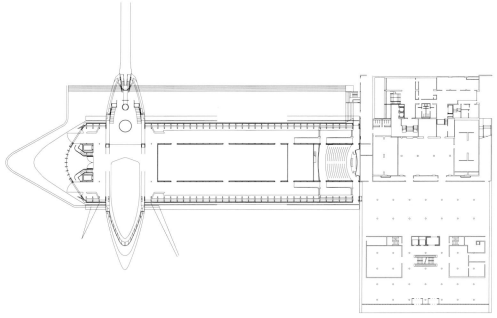

The aggressively sculptural and structurally daring work of Spanish-born architect and engineer Santiago Calatrava has long been a favorite of other architects. In recent years, Calatrava has won high-profile commissions—including the 2004 Olympic Sports Complex in Athens and a transit center

at the World Trade Center site in New York—that have elevated him from a designer of bridges, for which he first won acclaim, to a creator of landmark buildings. His first completed project in the United States made quite a splash: an addition to a 1957 Eero Saarinen–designed art museum in Milwaukee that soars above the shore of Lake Michigan like a massive but elegant prehistoric bird. ___ The avian analogy is apt: The large steel brise-soleil that shades a towering skylight above a reception hall—composed of seventy-two pairs of white steel fins hinged on a steel spine—opens and closes like the flapping wings of a huge bird. (Flapping is an exaggeration: It takes approximately four minutes for hydraulic lifts to open and close the massive structure.) The $1.5 million brise-soleil is the building's defining element and a landmark for the Rust Belt city of Milwaukee. ___ Calatrava's 58,000-square-foot (5,388-square-meter) addition extends to the south of the existing Saarinen structure, a combination art museum and war memorial with a Brutalist 1970s addition. The entrance to the entire complex is now in the Calatrava structure, which is reached by a pedestrian bridge with a towering mast and cable stays that echo the angular lines of the brise-soleil structure. The axial bridge spans 246 feet (75 meters) over a roadway to connect the city's main commercial street to the lakefront museum. The lobby is really an elliptical reception hall crowned by the angular skylight and brise-soleil. To the south of the entry hall is a meeting room and an outdoor terrace; to the north is a long gallery flanked by two narrower gallerias; a gift shop and auditorium are situated at the far end, adjoining the original Saarinen building, which is now given over entirely to gallery space. Running along the west side of the gallerias is an outdoor terrace. Beneath the reception hall is underground parking. ___ The central gallery and adjoining gallerias are defined by a series of closely spaced curving concrete ribs that taper down toward the edges of the building. Skylights between the arches fill the gallerias with daylight, while the central gallery must rely entirely on artificial illumination. The arches or ribs continue the curving geometry that permeates Calatrava's creation, from the exterior to the structure of the underground parking garage. These organic forms create a coherent, integrated whole. ___ Calatrava's striking addition is more of a giant entry piece for the older, more restrained Saarinen structure than a museum in its own right—although it adds 12,000 square feet (1,115 square meters) of exhibition space. The structure is an attention-getting entry piece that gives a strong new visual identity to an institution previously lacking one. Calatrava's landmark design also puts Milwaukee on the cultural destination map. ___ Below: Sections. ___ Opposite, top: Calatrava's sculpturally expressive addition to Eero Saarinen's original building hovers over the Lake Michigan shoreline like a giant prehistoric bird. ___ Opposite, bottom: Floor plan, with Calatrava addition at left.

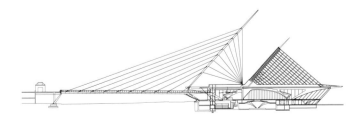

Above: The addition extends from the central atrium back toward Saarinen's rectilinear structure from 1957. —— Opposite, top: The giant brise-soleil sweeping over the large skylight at the heart of Calatrava's addition folds down, like the wings of a bird. —— Opposite, bottom: The addition's 12,000-square-foot volume contains a gallery, two gallerias, a gift shop, and an auditorium. —— Page 160: Sweeping arches support the underside of the structure. —— Page 161, top: The entrance to the museum is now situated in Calatrava's addition, which features sleek white surfaces. —— Page 161, bottom: The museum's wide-ranging permanent collection is spread throughout the original Saarinen building.

The riverfront town of Henley on Thames in southeast England is sacred ground in the world of rowing. Since it was founded in 1839, hundreds of crews from around the world have come to the small Oxfordshire town to compete in the nineteen or so races of the Henley Royal Regatta held each June.

David Chipperfield Architects	1998
River & Rowing Museum	
Henley on Thames, UK	

Henley's River and Rowing Museum asked British minimalist David Chipperfield to design "an astonishing museum" to house collections of rowing vessels and other artifacts. Of course, the setting for the building was right on the banks of the River Thames. ___ Chipperfield's design is not eye-popping; rather, it is a subtle Modernist interpretation of wooden sheds along the riverbank. The project houses three permanent galleries devoted to exhibitions about the sport of rowing, the Thames River, and the town of Henley, as well as special exhibition galleries, a café, a gift shop, an education center, a library, and various function rooms. ___ The architect divided the program into two main volumes: a boxy, two-story pavilion housing the education center on the ground floor and the library and one of the permanent exhibition spaces above, and a larger structure housing the two larger permanent exhibition spaces inside long gabled gallery volumes. On the ground floor, beneath the galleries, are the lobby, administrative offices, and temporary exhibition spaces, as well as a gift shop and a café that opens onto a wooden deck overlooking the river. Both structures are raised slightly above the ground on shallow concrete columns; both are finished in a subtle, elegant palette of exposed concrete, glass, and naturally weathered oak battens with turn-coated steel roofs. ___ The Rowing Gallery displays a collection of vessels varying from those used in ancient Greece to high-speed boats featured in the 2000 Sydney Olympics. There is also a Hall of Fame with the sport's greatest figures. The softly daylit gallery's narrow linear proportions are perfectly suited to the long, lean profiles of the boats and oars displayed on the floors, walls, and even ceilings. Chipperfield's design creates a cool, soothing mood—rather like contemplating a calm river. The Thames Gallery, the largest of the permanent exhibition areas, documents the wildlife, archaeology, and history of the river with photographs, paintings, and actual boats. Like the rowing exhibition space, Chipperfield designed the Thames Gallery as a linear space with vaulted ceilings that illuminate the interior through long skylights overhead. The Henley Gallery, which traces the history of the town from its founding in the twelfth century, has a completely different character: Connected to the other galleries by a long glass-enclosed bridge at the second level, the space is a more traditional box, with a wall of windows to bring in light instead of top-lit angular ceilings. ___ The structures have the look of streamlined modern versions of rustic Oxfordshire barns and riverside sheds. But there is added subtlety: Chipperfield has energized the Modernist sheds by cladding the upper levels in solid timber, so that they seem to float above the floor-to-ceiling expanses of glass along the first floor, which are shaded by simple white canopies. There is also a palpable Japanese quality to the structures—probably because Chipperfield honed his take on Eastern-infused Minimalism while working in Japan early in his career. Regardless of its exact pedigree, Chipperfield's building is a calming, appropriate addition to the Henley riverfront and one of the museum's best assets. ___ Opposite: The wooden sheds of the rowing museum blend innocuously into their riverside setting.

163

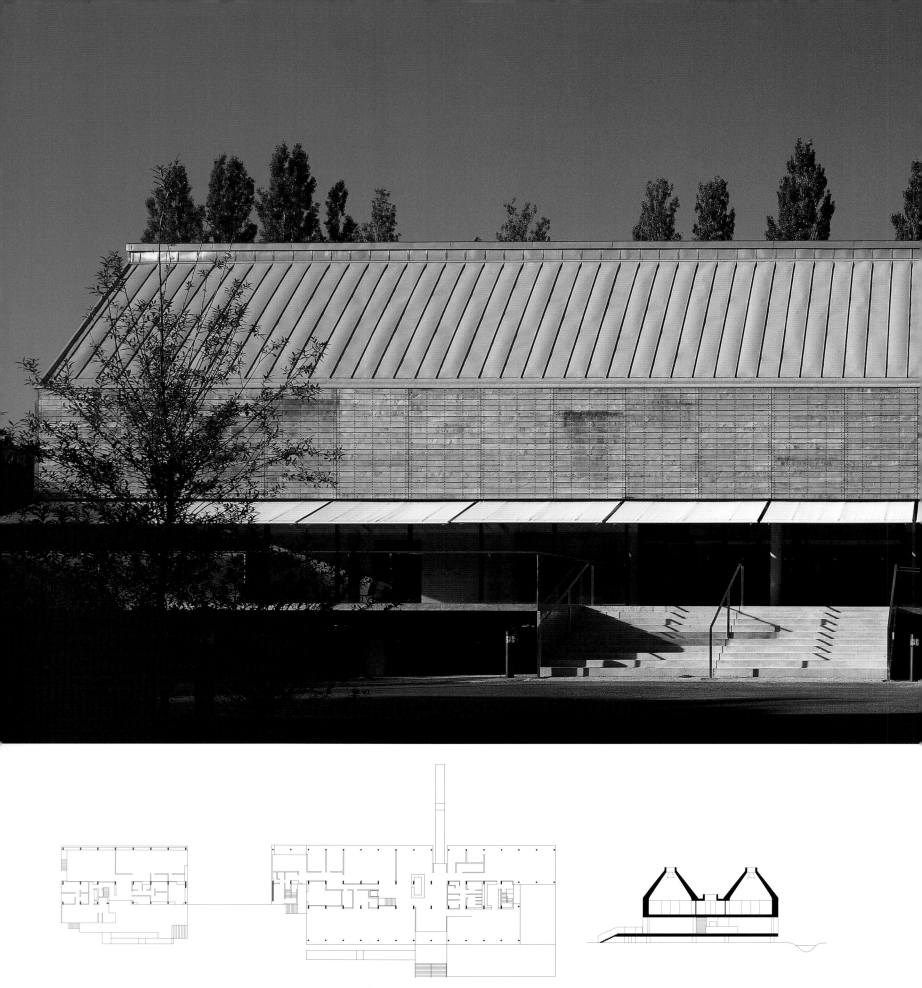

Above: A long ramp with a glass balustrade leads up to the museum's entrance. _____ Opposite, from left: Floor plan; section through galleries.

Above: The bridge creates a portal for the riverside museum. ____ Opposite, top: A glass-enclosed bridge connects the main gallery wing with a separate education center and library wing. ____ Opposite, bottom left: The two-story education wing is a simple timber-clad box that contrasts with the gabled galleries. ____ Opposite, bottom right: The ground floor of the gallery wing is wrapped in glass—a stark contrast to the timber walls and decking.

Above, left: The top-floor galleries enjoy daylight from windows along the perimeter and from skylights along the spine of the gabled roof. —— Above, right: Head-on views of the surrounding landscape make the museum's waterside setting part of the interior. —— Opposite, top: In one of the gallery spaces, a wall of floor-to-ceiling glass contrasts with a narrow glazed band along the opposite wall. —— Opposite, bottom left: Broad expanses of glass insides the gallery wing open up the interiors to daylight and views. A top-lit stair hall reveals the sleek minimalism for which Chipperfield is known. —— Opposite, bottom right: Low-lying galleries and glazed walls draw the eye into the surrounding landscape.

The Amsterdam-based practice UN Studio, headed by husband-and-wife team Ben van Berkel and Caroline Bos, designed the Het Valkhof Museum as a showcase for Holland's ancient past. The museum, located in the eastern Dutch town of Nijmegen, consolidates three existing museums devoted to

van Berkel & Bos	1999
Het Valkhof Museum	
Nijmegen, The Netherlands	

archaeology, pre-twentieth-century art, and modern art under a single roof. The architects combined these disparate institutions within a simple, barlike structure on the eastern side of a large public plaza in the center of Nijmegen, one of the first Roman settlements in what is now The Netherlands. The building creates a sleek, contemporary container for important artifacts from Dutch history. ____ The museum is not a large structure: It covers just 94,668 square feet (8,800 square meters) over two floors and a basement level. But it is a long, linear building, and so commands an important position on the tapered public plaza, which is surrounded by existing buildings on one side and parkland on the other two. ____ As in a classical building, the ground floor is the building's base or *piano rustica*, not its main public level. The ground floor houses the museum's more functional areas: a shop, education rooms, archives, storage, an auditorium, a café, and offices. A broad staircase just inside the lobby leads up to the main exhibition level on the second floor, where van Berkel & Bos arranged galleries like parallel streets. There are loftlike spaces devoted to Old Masters paintings, archaeology, and modern art, as well as areas for revolving exhibitions. The basement level, where an archaeological dig is framed in a courtyard, contains space for future expansion next to an installation workshop. ____ On the outside, the museum gives the initial impression of being a monolithic glass wall—a precisely etched iceberg—holding down an entire edge of the vast plaza in front of it. Compared to the commercial shop fronts lining the southern edge of the plaza, the museum is indeed a neutral container. But van Berkel & Bos gave the building subtle tweaks to make a livelier, more complex design. For instance, the main facade transforms subtly along its length from ribbons of sandblasted glass with depth and shadow to clear windows that open up diagonal views of the parkland behind. The facade's detailing suggests a much taller building. The architects divided the gallery level into three bands, which are then subdivided by thin horizontal mullions. Instead of a single story, the gallery floor looks like three levels. ____ Inside, the architects continue to subtly tweak straight lines with an undulating ceiling of slatted aluminum that conceals lighting, ductwork, and other infrastructure beneath a topographically varied surface. The ceiling seems to echo the rolling hillside visible just outside, which van Berkel & Bos made part of the indoors by lining the exterior walls with large expanses of floor-to-ceiling glass. ____ Throughout the museum, van Berkel & Bos's design creates a lively tension between dense European streetscapes and a natural landscape, between the messy remnants of ancient history and a more streamlined, orderly sense of modernity. More importantly, the partners balance the neutral box with nuance. As a result, the museum benefits from appropriately neutral spaces for art and artifacts but also connects the building to a larger physical and historical context. ____ Below: Transverse section. ____ Opposite: The striated skin on the museum's entry facade separates into ribbonlike layers that suggest multiple floor levels.

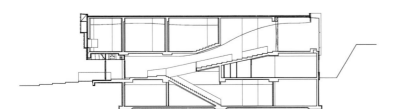

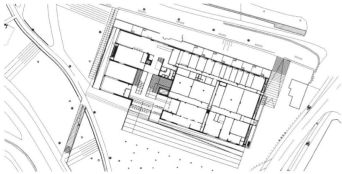

Above: Diagram showing possible circulation through the galleries. ___ Top left: The museum's northwest corner reveals the stepped profile and repetitive horizontal mullions of the curtain wall, which gives added height to the two-story structure. ___ Top right: The back side of the museum opens onto a wooded parkland. ___ Opposite, top: The main facade defines the eastern side of a large public plaza. ___ Opposite, bottom: At night, the apparently solid upper level becomes a glowing translucent skin.

Above: Broad steps lead up to the second-floor galleries. Large expanses of windows overlook the wooded landscape behind the museum. ⎯ Opposite, top right: Views of the landscape become part of the gallery interiors. ⎯ Opposite, bottom right: A louvered ceiling creates an undulating profile above the galleries.

Before expanding into new quarters by Álvaro Siza—a Pritzker Prize–winning architect known for his restrained monochromatic compositions of sunlight on whitewashed walls—the Serralves Foundation in Porto, Portugal, operated from distinctly different surroundings. The foundation, which

Álvaro Siza	1999
Serralves Museum	
Porto, Portugal	

collects post-1960 art, was previously housed in a pink Art Deco mansion built for the Count of Vizela in the 1930s, surrounded by impeccably landscaped parkland on the edge of the city. (Siza designed the seven-acre landscape immediately surrounding his new building to blend into the larger park and its mature vegetation.) Now Portugal's first large-scale contemporary art museum has an elegant and expansive building designed by Siza (a native of Porto) that seamlessly embraces both modernity and tradition. ___ Siza sited the 161,400-square-foot (15,000-square-meter) museum to preserve the physical and visual qualities of Serralves Park. The building keeps a relatively consistent roofline above the natural north-south slope of the site—a significant difference of 29.5 feet (9 meters) between top and bottom. Although there are actually two structures comprising the museum—a main U-shaped gallery block and a separate auditorium—Siza weaves them together into a continuous whole bound by walls of granite and stucco and punctuated by outdoor courtyards between various portions of the two structures. These courtyards are classic Siza: austere outdoor rooms defined by whitewashed walls that create a brilliant play of light, with stark floors of grass or earth-colored gravel punctuated by the occasional strategically placed tree. ___ Visitors enter the museum proper at the north end, having arrived on foot from Serralves Park or from the subterranean parking garage. The path to the entrance follows a shaded granite-paved walkway bordering the courtyard between the museum and the freestanding 300-seat auditorium where lectures, conferences, and music, theater, and dance performances are held. Inside, the lobby opens onto a soaring double-height atrium crowned by an immense skylight. This cool, light-washed space sets the tone for the remaining galleries, which extend southward from the atrium in two asymmetrical wings. Behind the atrium is a two-story art library with a reading room and study area; upstairs are a cafeteria, an eighty-seat dining room, and an open-air café overlooking the park. ___ There is no singular defining space in Siza's museum: Nearly every gallery, courtyard, and even corridor offers some rich spatial experience. The real star of the show is light. Just as he manipulates sunlight and shadow on the exteriors of the white stucco–clad volumes, Siza controls daylight inside to dazzling effect. Many of the galleries feature one of the architect's signatures: light-diffusing elements that resemble truncated Parsons tables. These inverted "tables" hang from the ceiling beneath skylights, evenly diffusing daylight and concealed artificial light over the suspended white surfaces and to the gallery's perimeter. (These devices also cleverly conceal air conditioning equipment.) The effect is a smooth wash of blended natural and artificial illumination that renders the whole room a luminous space. ___ These glowing galleries are not detached from the museum's physical surroundings. A number of them flank long circulation corridors with huge windows overlooking the museum's outdoor spaces, bringing the outside in and breaking up so much radiant abstraction. Indeed, that is part of Siza's genius: He creates buildings that seem to glow in an otherworldly light, but keeps them very much anchored to their setting and to history. ___ **Below: Elevation.** ___ **Opposite: Siza's design for the Serralves Museum weaves simple whitewashed forms into a lushly landscaped urban park.**

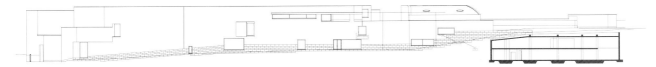

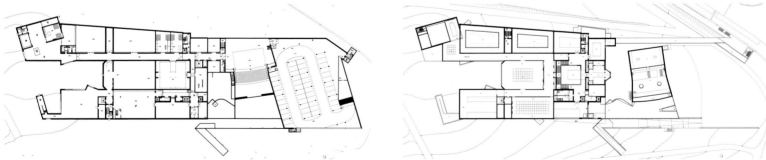

Above: Site plans. ___ Top: The long gallery wings follow the site's slope from north to south. ___ Opposite, top: A ramp leads into the museum complex, which is enclosed by walls of granite and stucco. ___ Opposite, center: The blank whitewashed wall of the auditorium block defines the northern edge of the museum precinct. ___ Opposite, bottom: Opposite the museum's north end, the other side of the auditorium frames an internal courtyard.

Above, left: Huge sliding windows in an exhibition space open onto the grassy courtyard. ___ Above, right: The entry foyer leads to a skylit double-height atrium. ___ Top: Siza's masterful control of natural and artificial lighting gives the museum's galleries a distinct glow. ___ Opposite: A projecting window bay along one of the gallery wings animates the smooth white surfaces of Siza's minimalist composition.

Amsterdam architect Abel Cahen undertook a renovation—and radical reimagining—of the Van Abbemuseum in Eindhoven, one of The Netherlands' leading collections of modern and contemporary art. Before the addition, the museum, housed in a landmark red brick structure built by the architect A.J.

Abel Cahen	2003
Van Abbemuseum	
Eindhoven, The Netherlands	

Kropholler in 1936 with a quaint bell tower, was bursting at the seams. The collection of roughly 2,700 works—from Pablo Picasso and Marc Chagall to Frank Stella and Joseph Beuys, among other artists—had grown tremendously in recent years; so had the museum's library and its staff. Besides space, the existing facility was sorely lacking in modern amenities for the public. So the institution commissioned Cahen and Belgian interior designer Maarten van Severen to create an entirely new wing with sorely needed exhibition space, an auditorium, an education center, a library, a café, and a shop. Cahen renovated the original 1936 building and added a new wing that leaves no question as to its vintage. ___ Nothing about the Van Abbemuseum's expansion was subtle. Even its site, behind Eindhoven's City Hall on the River Dommell, was altered by landscape designers HNS of Utrecht, who widened the river and added fishing terraces overlooking the water. The addition's angular placement next to the existing building frames a smaller "lake." The museum's new restaurant takes advantage of this sheltered spot with an outdoor dining patio that points into the river like the prow of a small ship. ___ Visitors access the museum through the original entry and descend a grand staircase to a subterranean foyer connecting the new and old wings. The original building contains renovated galleries; new public facilities, such as the restaurant and auditorium, are located in the two-story wing, along with new gallery space. The new building's distinguishing feature is a 88.5-foot (27-meter) tower that overshadows the original bell tower in height and girth. The hefty, angular tower organizes circulation space within the addition. Inside is a large studio and exhibition space where visiting artists can set up shop. Maarten van Severen, who has created furniture for Vitra and collaborated with Rem Koolhaas, designed the interior of the auditorium, the shop (with acid-green floors), the restaurant, the educational center, and the public library, one of the most dramatic new spaces. The sleek, luminous library, with a collection of 120,000 objects and archives, spreads out over three floors that wind around a towering atrium. Cahen designed these new functions to operate independently of the museum itself, thereby creating a lively cultural hub with a life of its own beyond the museum's operating hours. ___ Cahen faced the new exterior not in red brick, but gray slate from Lapland. The monochromatic skin has a variegated, almost pixilated quality brought out by subtle differences in the square stone panels. Depending on the light and weather, the exterior changes from silvery gray to a dark anthracite color. It may sound like an obtrusive addition to a genteel historic landmark, but Cahen's new wing adds a much-needed jolt of energy to an important but overlooked institution. Its aggressive forms and interiors actually respect the original building: there's no mistaking new and old in this lively new complex. ___ Opposite: The new gallery wing, which extends into the widened River Dommell, is clad in gray slate from Lapland.

Above, left and right: A large skylight illuminates galleries surrounding a stair tower in the new addition. ___ Opposite, top: A curving glass wall creates a knuckle between the original 1936 building and the new library wing. ___ Opposite, bottom: Cahen and Belgian interior designer Maarten van Severen created luminous, minimalist interiors that play with subtle changes in textures and materials. ___ Page 184, top: The expansion includes an auditorium and gallery wing, dominated by an angular tower, and a library and educational center that can operate independently of the museum. ___ Page 184, bottom: The pixilated pattern of slate cladding the addition animates its windowless surfaces. ___ Page 185, top: The slate-clad expansion distinguishes itself from the brick exterior of the museum's original 1936 building, at right. ___ Page 185, bottom: Walls of limestone and glass frame an outdoor courtyard of water.

One of Steven Holl's most important projects is Kiasma, a contemporary art museum in Helsinki. When it opened in 1998, it was one of the New York architect's largest built works, and an important expression of the longtime theorist's vision. Holl, who bested more than 500 entrants in a

Steven Holl Architects	1998
Kiasma Museum of Contemporary Art	
Helsinki, Finland	

1992 competition to win the commission, named his design after a Finnish word that refers to the crossing of two lines or an intertwining. ___ The building, properly known as the Helsinki Museum of Contemporary Art, occupies a prominent site in the center of town. The museum sits between the Finnish parliament building to the west, Eliel Saarinen's stern, imposing Helsinki Station to the east, and Alvar Aalto's Finlandia Hall to the north. Kiasma's site is defined on two sides by a busy thoroughfare and by Töölo Bay on the third. The intertwining suggested by the nickname Kiasma occurs in the building's plan, where two gently curving ribbons of space merge, and in section, as orthogonal and curved geometries overlay each other to generate a strikingly fluid, unfamiliar but graceful form. Holl also sees the building's irregular mass as intertwining with the geometry of the city and landscape. ___ One enters the museum by passing between two long bar structures that define the ground floor's peculiar geometric form, a bookshop and café to the left, a classroom to the right. Wedged between these two wings, the entry opens into the museum's most dramatic space: a soaring curved hall with a black concrete ramp arcing up to the galleries. An arched translucent roof washes the gracefully tapered hall in cool Nordic light. ___ Indeed, manipulating daylight is one of the central ideas behind Holl's design. In Helsinki's far northern latitude, the sunlight is weak and almost always at a low angle, so reflecting daylight is key to creating luminous interiors. Holl used the building's geometry to get natural light into all of the twenty-five galleries. The museum's west wall brings in daylight through glass panels with translucent insulation, allowing galleries below the top floor to receive natural light. In the top-floor galleries, light filters in from two directions: through a clerestory along the center of the building and via curving skylights above the gentle vault of the museum's roof. The galleries vary in size and shape throughout the building, which Holl describes as a "gallery of rooms." ___ Light may be one of the building's most important materials, but it is certainly not the only one. While he has kept the interiors generally neutral—plaster walls and stained concrete floors—Holl has used a variety of elements on the exterior: concrete, sandblasted glass, weathered zinc, brushed aluminum, and acid-reddened brass. The effect is not chaotic, but rich and engaging. The building's complex, intertwined geometry makes it impossible to understand as a single object—so one sees it as a constantly unfolding entity as one moves around it. Holl uses the range of materials on its ever-changing facades for particular effects. In the staid, stoic landscape of central Helsinki, Kiasma's complex intertwining makes for a richly nuanced building. ___ Opposite: The northwest facade mixes geometries and materials, including glass, weathered zinc, and acid-reddened brass.

Above: The museum's long, ribbonlike massing weaves together orthogonal and curving geometries that respond to the intertwining between the building and the urban landscape. —— Opposite, top right: An extruded canopy marks the entrance on the south facade. —— Opposite, bottom right: Along the northeastern part of the angled form, skylights peeled out of the curved, standing-seam zinc skin bring daylight into top-floor galleries. —— Opposite, left: Floor plans.

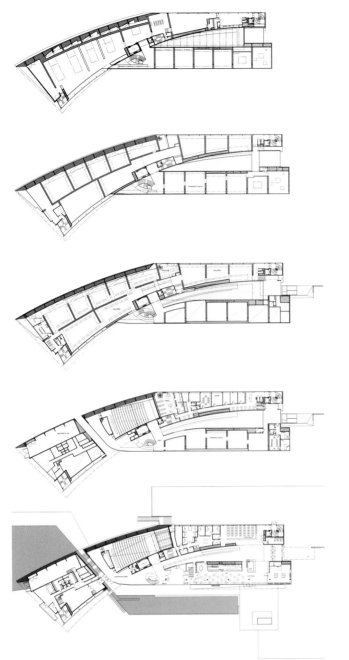

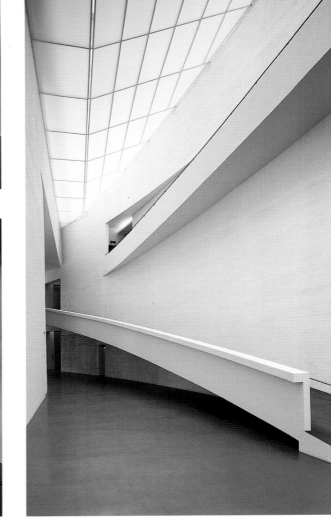

Above: A sinuous spiraling staircase, which echoes the profile of the atrium ramp, begins at the second floor and joins the gallery levels. —— Opposite, top left: The galleries combine natural and artificial light, both of which are modulated by lowered ceiling planes. —— Opposite, center left: Galleries feature dark gray concrete floors, whitewashed walls, and artificial lighting recessed in long troughs to create softer, more even illumination. —— Opposite, bottom left: In the top-floor galleries, skylights in the curving roof bring in daylight despite the low sun angle. —— Opposite, right: The dramatic skylit atrium is dominated by a gently sweeping ramp leading up to gallery levels. Behind the solid wall is the theater.

For all of the additions and alterations by esteemed modern architects it has undergone during its 75-year history, the Museum of Modern Art has never identified itself with a signature work of architecture. MoMA's masterpieces have always left more lasting impressions than its buildings by

Philip L. Goodwin and Edward Durell Stone, Philip Johnson, and Cesar Pelli, stitched together over the years in the middle of a Midtown Manhattan block. ____ MoMA's long-awaited $425 million expansion and renovation by Japanese architect Yoshio Taniguchi, which opened in November 2004, will not appease those looking for the museum to unveil a landmark. Taniguchi, who worked with executive architect Kohn Pedersen Fox Associates of New York, says he approached the commission as an urban design project, creating a museum within a city rather than a building with a distinctive architectural identity. His plan restores the 1939 Goodwin and Stone building and 1965 Johnson wing and weaves them together with the base of Cesar Pelli's 1984 Museum Tower and two new wings that frame Johnson's iconic Abby Aldrich Rockefeller sculpture garden as an important nexus. ____ Taniguchi's deft weaving of old and new is clearly evident along the West 53rd Street elevation, where his own architecture quietly continues the panorama of the museum's history revealed in the conjoined facades by previous architects. On the West 54th Street facade, Taniguchi has used serene, subdued materials—mainly clear, gray, and frit-patterned glass—to unify a new gallery wing and education and research center, due to open in 2006, that quietly frame the restored and expanded sculpture garden. Despite their hushed palette, Taniguchi's new wings give a prominence within the city the old MoMA never enjoyed. The inverse is true, too: With large walls of glass along the gallery block, views of the Manhattan streetscapes are suddenly and forcefully brought into the exhibition spaces, linking the institution and the city in a new reciprocal relationship. ____ Taniguchi's expansion nearly doubles the space of the museum to a total of roughly 630,000 square feet (58,527 square meters) on six levels. The lobby now spans the full city block, with entrances on both West 53rd and 54th Streets. From there, visitors are funneled into an interior forecourt opening onto a view of the sculpture garden through a full-height wall of glass. The forecourt leads up a black granite staircase to the revamped MoMA's most striking new space, a towering 110-foot-tall atrium filled with natural light from overhead skylights and the great glass wall overlooking the garden. Taniguchi also created galleries for unconventional and large-scale contemporary works that would never have fit in the old MoMA's confined galleries. ____ Taniguchi's new MoMA may not have the knock-'em-dead architectural pyrotechnics some visitors have come to expect from big-name museums. That is entirely by design. Early on, Taniguchi told the MoMA trustees that if he were given a generous budget he would deliver great architecture; but if he had an even bigger budget he would make the architecture disappear. ____ Opposite: A view across West 54th Street shows how the new gallery wing, which faces the reinstalled sculpture garden, engages the base of the Cesar Pelli–designed Museum Tower.

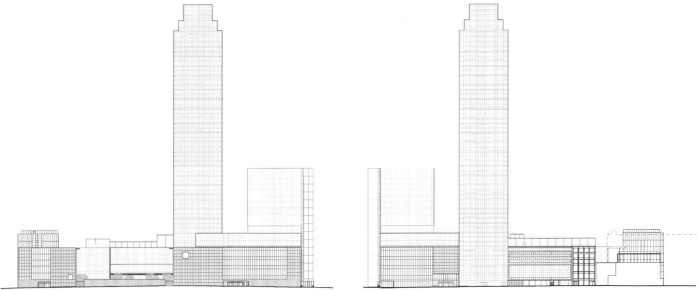

Above: A deep roof overhang above the east elevation of the new gallery wing creates a towering portico overlooking the sculpture garden. ___ Opposite, top: An aerial view of the museum's sculpture garden on West 54th Street shows that it has taken a central place in Taniguchi's redesign. ___ Opposite, bottom: Elevations. ___ Page 198, top: Taniguchi's 53rd Street facade joins (left to right) Cesar Pelli's 1984 Museum Tower, Goodwin and Stone's 1939 building, and Philip Johnson's 1964 addition. ___ Page 198, bottom: Ground-floor plan. ___ Page 199, top: On the third floor, a glass-lined corridor offers views back to the expanded gallery wing and the historic building facades along West 54th Street. ___ Page 199, bottom: Matisse's *Dance (I)* hangs above a sculptural staircase connecting the fourth- and fifth-floor galleries, with a view to the atrium.

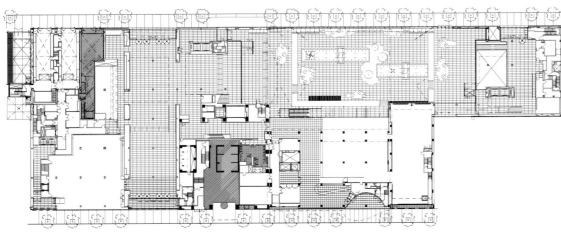

Above: The third-floor architecture and design galleries look out onto West 54th Street and the Philip Johnson–designed sculpture garden. —— Top: Visitors move through the building via staircases that lead to galleries and narrow bridges that connect them. —— Opposite: The towering 110-foot-tall atrium, dominated by Barnett Newman's imposing *Broken Obelisk*, offers glimpses of vertical circulation through the gallery wing and the lobby below.

Obayashi Corporation

Notes to Introduction

[1] Victoria Newhouse, *Towards A New Museum* (New York: Monacelli Press, 1998), p. 8.

[2] Ibid., p. 138.

[3] Ibid., p. 162.

[4] See *The New Yorker*, September 15, 2003.

[5] Maggie Toy, ed., *Architectural Design: Contemporary Museums* (London: Academy Editions/John Wiley & Sons Ltd., 1997), p. 94.

[6] James Steele, ed., *Museum Builders* (London: Academy Editions, 1994), p. 9.

[7] Ibid.

Project Credits

Gallery of Horyuji Treasures, Tokyo, Japan

Architect: Taniguchi & Associates, Tokyo, Japan —— Client: Ministry of Education and Ministry of Construction —— Landscape Architect: Kazumi Mizoguchi —— Engineer: Kozo Kaikaku Kenkyusho (structural)

Liner Museum, Appenzell, Switzerland

Architect: Gigon/Guyer, Zürich, Switzerland —— Client: Stiftung Carl Liner Vater und Sohn —— Engineer: Aerni+Aerni (civil) —— Contractor: Urs Birchmeier

Museo de Bellas Artes Castellón, Castellón de la Plana, Spain

Architect: Mansilla + Tuñón, Madrid, Spain —— Design Team: Clara Moreno, Andrés Regueiro, Matilde Peralta, María Linares, Jaime Prior, Andrés Rojo, Félix Larragueta, David Nadal, Fernando García-Pino, Jaime Gimeno, Katrien Vertenten, Gregory Peñate, Oscar F. Aguayo —— Client: Generalitat Valenciana —— Engineer: JG & Asociados, Alfonso Gomez Gaite —— Contractor: FCC Construcción, S.A.

Rosenthal Center for Contemporary Art, Cincinnati, Ohio, USA

Architect: Zaha Hadid Architects, London, UK —— Design Team: Ed Gaskin, Ana Sotrel, David Gerber, Jan Hübener, Christos Passas, Sonia Villaseca, James Lim, Jee-Eun Lee, Oliver Domeisen, Helmut Kinzler, Patrik Schumacher, Michael Wolfson, David Gomersall —— Engineers: Jane Wernick, THP Limited (structural), Heapy Engineering (mechanical/electrical)

Paper Art Museum, Shizuoka, Japan

Architect: Shigeru Ban Architects, Tokyo, Japan —— Design Team: Shigeru Ban, Nobutaka Hiraga, Tadahiro Kawano, Keina Ishioka —— Client: Tokushu Paper Mfg. Co., Ltd. —— Engineers: Hoshino Architect & Engineer (structural), Chiku Engineering Consultants (mechanical) —— Contractor:

Kunsthaus Graz, Graz, Austria

Architect: Peter Cook and Colin Fournier, Graz, Austria —— Design Team: Peter Cook and Colin Fournier, Niels Jonkhans, Mathis Osterhage, Marcos Cruz and team, Nicola Haines, Karim Hamza, Anja Leonhäuser, Jamie Nord New Yen —— Client: City of Graz —— Engineer: Bollinger und Grohmann (structural) —— Other: Kress und Adams (lighting)

Modern Art Museum of Fort Worth, Fort Worth, Texas, USA

Architect: Tadao Ando Architect & Associates, Osaka, Japan —— Design Team: Larry Burns, Peter Arendt, Rollie Childers, Nobuhiko Shoga, Jory Alexander —— Client: MPA Foundation —— Landscape Architect: SWA Group —— Engineers: Thornton-Tomasetti Engineers (structural), CHP & Associates (mechanical/ electrical) —— Contractor: Linbeck Construction Corporation —— Other: George Sexton Associates (lighting consultant), Peter M. Muller, Inc. (curtain wall), Cerami & Associates (acoustical consultant)

Great Court, British Museum, London, UK

Architect: Foster and Partners, London, UK —— Design Team: Norman Foster, Spencer de Grey, Giles Robinson, Michael Jones, Julia Abell, William Castagna, Mark Costello, Daniel Goldberg, Nesa Marojevic, Peter Matcham, Filo Russo, Paul Simms, Peter Vandendries, Oliver Wong, Diane Ziegler —— Client: Trustees of the British Museum —— Engineer: Buro Happold —— Contractor: MACE Ltd.

Schaulager, Basel, Switzerland

Architect: Herzog & de Meuron, Basel, Switzerland —— Design Team: Senta Adolf, Philippe Fürstenberger, Harry Gugger, Nicole Hatz, Jacques Herzog, Ines Huber, Jürgen Johner, Pierre de Meuron, Carmen Müller, Cornel Pfister, Katja Ritz, Marc Schmidt, Florian Stirnemann, Lukas Weber, Martin Zimmerli —— Client: Laurenz Stiftung —— Engineers: Zachmann + Pauli Bauinge-nieure (structural), Amstein & Walthert (lighting, mechanical) —— Contractor: GSG Projekt Partner

Imperial War Museum North, Manchester, UK

Architect: Studio Daniel Libeskind, New York, New York, USA —— Design Team: Martin Ostermann, Wendy James, Markus Aerni —— Client: Trustees of the Imperial War Museum —— Landscape Architect: Studio Daniel Libeskind —— Engineers: Arup (structural, civil), Mott MacDonald (services) —— Contractor: Sir Robert McAlpine, Ltd.

O Museum, Nigano, Japan

Architect: Kazuyo Sejima + Ryue Nishizawa/SANAA, Tokyo, Japan —— Design Team: Kazuyo Sejima, Ryue Nishizawa, Yoshitaka Tanase —— Client: Iida City, Japan ——

Engineers: Sasaki Structural Consultants (structural), ES Associates, Nichiei Architect (mechanical) —— Contractor: Ota Co., Ltd.

Vulcania Museum, St. Ours-les-Roches, France

Architect: Hans Hollein, Vienna, Austria —— Design Team: Prof. Hans Hollein, Hans-Peter Wunsch —— Client: Consell Régional d'Auvergne, Chamalières —— Landscape Architect: Acanthe, Paris; Gilles Clément, Pierre Déeat —— Engineers: BET ITC (structural), BET Choulet (mechanical)

Centre PasquArt, Biel, Switzerland

Architect: Diener & Diener Architekten, Basel, Switzerland —— Client: Centre PasquArt Foundation —— Landscape Architect: Kienast Vogt Partner —— Engineer: Dr. Mathys & Wysseier Ingenieur & Planer AG (construction) —— Light: Institut für Tageslichttechnik

Palmach Museum of History, Tel Aviv, Israel

Architect: Zvi Hecker, Tel Aviv, Israel —— Design Team: Zvi Hecker, Rafi Segal, H. Pomagrin, S. Nuorahcs —— Client: M. Peri, S. Gavish, Palmach Veterans Association —— Landscape Architect: Tichnun Nof Ltd. —— Engineers: Eisenberg Naginski Zeldin (structural), Tal Cohen Ltd. (electrical, HVA) —— Contractor: Solel Boneh Ltd.

American Folk Art Museum, New York, New York, USA

Architect: Tod Williams Billie Tsien & Associates, New York, New York, USA —— Design Team: Phillip Ryan, Jennifer Turner, Nina Hollein, Vivian Wang, Hana Kassem, Kyra Clarkson, Andy Kim, William Vincent, Leslie Hansen —— Client: American Folk Art Museum —— Engineers: Severud Associates (structural), Ambrosino, DePinto & Schmeider (mechanical) —— Contractor: Pavarini Construction

Jewish Museum, Berlin, Germany

Architect: Studio Daniel Libeskind, New York, New York, USA —— Design Team: Daniel Libeskind, Matthias Reese, Jan Dinnebier, Stefan Blach —— Client: Jewish Musem Berlin —— Landscape Architect: Müller, Knippschild, Wehberg —— Engineers: GSE Tragwerkplaner, IGW Ingenieurgruppe Wiese (structural), Cziesielski + Partner (civil)

Museum of Modern Art Ludwig Foundation, Vienna, Austria

Architect: Ortner & Ortner, Berlin, Germany —— Client: Museumsquartier Developing & Operating Co., Vienna —— Design Team: Laurids and Manfred Ortner, Christian Lichtenwagner —— Engineer: Fritsch, Chiari & Partner, Ziviltechniker GmbH —— Contractor: Philipp Holzmann/Ed Ast/Held & Francke

Museum of Hiroshige Ando, Bato, Japan

Architect: Kengo Kuma & Associates, Tokyo, Japan —— Design Team: Kengo Kuma, Shoji Oshio, Susumu Yasukouchi, Toshio Yada, Yasunori Sakano, Ryusuke Fujieda —— Client: Bato Municipal —— Engineers: Aoki Structural Engineers (structural), P.T. Morimura & Associates (mechanical) —— Contractor: Obayashi Corporation

Nasher Sculpture Center, Dallas, Texas, USA
Architect: Renzo Piano Building Workshop, Genoa, Italy ⎯⎯
Client: The Nasher Foundation ⎯⎯ Landscape Architect:
Peter Walker & Partners ⎯⎯ Engineer: Ove Arup & Partners
⎯⎯ Contractor: HC Beck

Altamira Museum, Santillana Del Mar, Spain
Architect: Juan Navarro Baldeweg, Madrid, Spain ⎯⎯
Design Team: Juan Navarro Baldeweg, Andrea Lupberger,
Alvaro Galmes, Jaime Breton Lesmes, Daniel Delbruck, Andrea
Kaiser, Andres Jaque Ovejero, Miguel Bernardini Asenjo,
Marcello Maugeri, Sibylle Streck ⎯⎯ Client: Consorcio Para
Altamira ⎯⎯ Engineers: MC-2 Julio Martinez Calzon (struc-
tural), Argu Ingenieria y Servicios (mechanical) ⎯⎯
Contractor: NECSO Entrecanales y Cubiertas

**Milwaukee Art Museum Addition, Milwaukee,
Wisconsin, USA**
Architect: Santiago Calatrava, Zürich, Switzerland ⎯⎯
Design Team: Santiago Calatrava, David Kahler ⎯⎯ Client:
Milwaukee Art Museum ⎯⎯ Landscape Architect: Dan
Kiley ⎯⎯ Engineer: Santiago Calatrava ⎯⎯ Contractor:
C.G. Schmidt

River & Rowing Museum, Henley on Thames, UK
Architect: David Chipperfield Architects, London, UK ⎯⎯
Design Team: Renato Benedetti, Peter Crompton, Rebecca
Elliot, Spencer Fung, Alec Gillies, Victoria Jessen-Pike, Harvey
Langston-Jones, Genevieve Lilley, Andrew Llowarch, Rik Nys,
John Onken, Peter Andreas Sattrup, Silvana Schulze, Maurice
Shapiro, Mechthild Stuhlmacher, Simon Timms ⎯⎯ Client:
The River & Rowing Museum Foundation ⎯⎯ Landscape
Architect: Whitelaw Turkington ⎯⎯ Engineers: Whitbybird
(structural), Furness Green Partners (Services) ⎯⎯
Contractors: Norwest Holst Construction Limited ⎯⎯ Other:
Davis Langdon Everest (quantity surveyor)

Het Valkhof Museum, Nijmegen, The Netherlands
Architect: van Berkel & Bos, UN Studio, Amsterdam, The
Netherlands ⎯⎯ Design Team: Ben van Berkel with Rob
Hootsmans, Henri Snel, Remco Bruggink, Hugo Beschoor Plug,
Walther Kloet, Marc Dijkman, Jacco van Wengerden, Luc Veeger,
Florian Fischer, Carsten Kiselowsky ⎯⎯ Client: Stichting
Museum Het Valkhof ⎯⎯ Landscape Architects: Bureau B&B,
Stedebouw en landschapsarchitectuur, Michael van Gessel ⎯⎯
Engineer: Adviesbureau voor Bouwtechniek ⎯⎯ Contractor:
Nelissen van Egteren Bouw

Serralves Museum of Contemporary Art, Porto, Portugal
Architect: Álvaro Siza, Porto, Portugal ⎯⎯ Design Team:
Clemente Menéres Semide (principal in charge); Tiago Faria
(1st phase); Christian Gaenshirt, Sofia Thenaisie Coelho
(2nd phase); Edison Okumura, Abílio Mourão, Avelino Silva,
João Sabugueiro, Cristina Ferreirinha, Taichi Tomuro, Daniela
Antonucci, Francesca Montalto, Francisco Reina Guedes, Ulrich
Krauss, Angela Princiotto (3rd phase) ⎯⎯ Client: Serralves
Foundation ⎯⎯ Landscape Architects: João Gomes da Silva,
Erika Shakar ⎯⎯ Engineers: João Maria Sobreira, Raul

Serafim, Alexandre Martins, Inês Sobreira, Raquel Fernandes,
GET Alfredo Costa Pereira ⎯⎯ Contractor: Edifer

Van Abbemuseum, Eindhoven, The Netherlands
Architect: Abel Cahen, Amsterdam, The Netherlands ⎯⎯
Design Team: Paul van Berkum, Wouter Deen, Leo Krüse, Naud
Schroeder ⎯⎯ Client: Municipality of Eindhoven ⎯⎯
Landscape Architect: H+N+S Landscape Architects ⎯⎯
Engineers: Adviesbureau Tielemans Bouwconstructies (structural),
Nelissen Ingenieurs Bureau (insulation) ⎯⎯ Contractor:
Bouwcombinatie Hurks-Van Straaten

Kiasma Museum of Contemporary Art, Helsinki, Finland
Architect: Steven Holl Architects, New York, New York, USA
⎯⎯ Client: Finnish Ministry of Education ⎯⎯ Engineers:
Insinööritoimisto OY Matti Ollila & Co. Consulting Engineers
(structural), Tauno Nissinen OY Consulting Engineering (electrical), Ove Arup & Partners Consulting Engineers, PC (structural,
mechanical) ⎯⎯ Contractor: Seicon OY

Museum of Modern Art, New York, New York, USA
Architect: Taniguchi & Associates, Tokyo, Japan ⎯⎯
Executive Architect: Kohn Pedersen Fox & Associates, 111
West 57th Street, New York, New York, 10019 ⎯⎯ Design
Team: Yoshio Taniguchi, Brain Aamoth, Peter Hahn, Keiji
Ogawa, Taichi Tomuro, Junko Imamura ⎯⎯ Client: Museum
of Modern Art ⎯⎯ Engineers: Sevrud Associates and Guy
Nordenson and Associates (structural) Altieri Sebor Wieber
(mechanical) ⎯⎯ Landscape Architect: Zion Breen and
Richardson Associates ⎯⎯ Contractor: AMEC New York
⎯⎯ Other: George Sexton Associates (lighting), R.H.
Heintges Architects (facades)

Further Reading

Andelini, Luigi and Ruggero Baldasso, *Mansilla + Tuñón*. Milan:
Elemond Electa, 2000.

Ando, Tadao, Kenneth Frampton, and Massimo Vignelli, *Tadao
Ando: Light and Water*. New York: Monacelli Press, 2003.

Baldeweg, Juan Navarro and Juan Manuel Bonet, *Juan Navarro
Baldeweg*. San Francisco: Gingko Press, 2001.

Bognar, Botond and Kengo Kuma, *Kengo Kuma: Selected Works*.
New York: Princeton Architectural Press, 2005.

Buchanan, Peter, *Renzo Piano Building Workshop: Complete
Works, Vols. 1–4*. London: Phaidon Press, 1999–2003.

Chipperfield, David, *David Chipperfield*. New York: Princeton
Architectural Press, 2003.

Cook, Peter and Colin Fournier, *A Friendly Alien: Ein Kunsthaus
fur Graz*. Ostfildern, Germany: Hatje Cantz Publishers, 2004.

Dal Co, Francesco, *Tadao Ando: Complete Works*, London:
Phaidon Press, reprint edition, 1997.

Frampton, Kenneth, *Alvaro Siza*. London: Phaidon Press, 2000.

Garofalo, Francesco, *Steven Holl*. New York: Universe, 2003.

Gigon, Annette, Mike Guyer, and Edelbert Kob, *Annette
Gigon/Mike Guyer: Museum Liner Appenzell*. Ostfildern,
Germany: Hatje Cantz Publishers, 2001.

Hadid, Zaha, Paul Warchol, and Hélène Binet, *Zaha Hadid:
Space for Art—Contemporary Arts Center, Cincinnati*. Baden,
Switzerland: Lars Müller Publishers, 2004.

Hollein, Hans and Joseph Kosuth, *New Museology*. New York:
St. Martin's Press, 1992.

Jenkins, David, *Norman Foster Works: 1 & 4*. New York: Prestel
Publishing, 2003–2005.

Kieren, Mark and Christian Vogt, *Diener and Diener Architects:
Buildings and Projects, 1981–1996*. Basel: Birkhäuser Verlag,
1996.

Mack, Gerhard, *Herzog & De Meuron: the Complete Works (vols.
1–3)*. Basel: Birkhäuser, 1997–2005.

McQuaid, Matilda, *Shigeru Ban*. London: Phaidon Press, 2003.

Ortner, Laurids, *Ortner & Ortner: 3 Buildings for European
Culture*. Cologne: Verlag Der Buchhandlung Walther Konig,
1999.

Pare, Richard, *Tadao Ando: The Colours of Light*. London:
Phaidon Press, 2000.

Sejima, Kazuyo and Ryue Nishizawa, *Kazuyo Sejima + Ryue
Nishizawa/SANAA: Works 1995–2003*. Tokyo: Toto, 2003.

Schneider, Bernhard and Daniel Libeskind, *Daniel Libeskind
Jewish Museum Berlin: Between the Lines*. New York: Prestel
Publishing, 1999.

Taniguchi, Yoshio and Glenn Lowry, *The New Museum of Modern
Art*. New York: Museum of Modern Art, 2005.

Taniguchi, Yoshio and Terence Riley, *Nine Museums*. New York:
Museum of Modern Art, 2004.

Tzonis, Alexander, *Santiago Calatrava: Complete Works*. New
York: Rizzoli, 2004.

van Berkel, Ben, Caroline Bos, and Aaron Betsky, *UN Studio:
UNFOLD*. Rotterdam: NAI Publishers, 2002.

Williams, Tod, Billie Tsien, Michael Moran, and Hadley Arnold,
Work/Life : Tod Williams Billie Tsien. New York: Monacelli
Press, 2001.

Index

Photo Credits

All illustrations were generously provided by the architects, unless otherwise specified. Photographic sources are listed whenever possible, but the publisher will endeavor to rectify any inadvertent omissions.

© Bitter + Bredt: p80; pp82–87; p120; pp122–127
© Tom Bonner: p7tr
© Richard Bryant/Arcaid: p162; pp164–169
© Jimmy Cohrssen: p7tl; p10tr
© Michael Denancé: p144; pp145–149
Courtesy Dia Art Foundation: p11tl
© Mitsumasa Fujitsuka: p136; pp138–143
Courtesy Michael Graves & Associates: p13tl
© Roland Halbe: p36; p39; p40–43; pp102/3; p150; pp152–155; p176; pp178–181
© Hiroyuki Hirai: p44; p46–49
© Timothy Hursley: p156; p159; pp160/1; p194; pp196–201
© Rudolf Klein: p113
Courtesy Rem Koolhaas/Office For Metropolotan Architecture (OMA): p9tl; p13c
© Michael Krüger: p106; p108–112
Kunsthaus Graz/LMJ Graz/Niki Lackner: p50; pp52–54; pp56/7
© Jannes Linders: p182; p184t; p185t
Peter Mackinven/V&A Images: p9tr
© Mitsuo Matsuoka/Tadao Ando Architect & Associates: pp58–65
© Michael Moran: p114; pp116–119
© Christian Richters: p170; pp172–175
© Shinkenchiku-sha: p14; p16–21; p88; pp90–93
© Margherita Spillutini: p10tl; p72; pp74–79
© Rupert Steiner: p128; pp130–135
© Paul Warchol Photography, Inc.: p188; pp190–193
© Gaston Wicky: p100; pp104/5
© Nigel Young/Foster and Partners: p66; pp68–71

Phaidon Press Limited
Regent's Wharf
All Saints Street
London N1 9PA

Phaidon Press Inc.
180 Varick Street
New York, NY 10014

www.phaidon.com

First published 2005
© 2005 Phaidon Press Limited

ISBN: 0 7148 4498 5

A CIP catalogue record for this book is available from
the British Library.

Designed by Jenny 8 Del Corte Hirschfeld + Mischa Leiner/
CoDe. Communication and Design
Printed in Hong Kong